Illustrated BUYER'S ★ GUIDE™

VOLKSWAGEN

Peter Vack

MBI Publishing Company

Dedication

This book is dedicated to my three daughters, Michelle, Grace, and Yvette.

First published in 1998 by MBI Publishing Company, 729 Prospect Avenue, PO Box 1, Osceola, WI 54020-0001 USA

MBI Publishing Company books are also available at discounts in bulk quantity for industrial or sales-promotional use. For details write to Special Sales Manager at Motorbooks International Wholesalers & Distributors, 729 Prospect Avenue, PO Box 1, Osceola, WI 54020-0001 USA.

Library of Congress Cataloging-in-Publication Data
Vack, Peter.
    Illustrated buyer's guide. Volkswagen/Peter Vack.
        p. cm.
    New ed. of: Illustrated Volkswagen buyer's guide/Peter Vack.
1993
    Includes index.
    ISBN 0-7603-0574-9 (pbk.: alk. paper)
    1. Volkswagen automobiles—Purchasing. I. Vack, Peter.
    Illustrated Volkswagen buyer's guide. Ii. Title.
TL215.V6V32   1998
629.222'2—dc21   98-34751

On the front cover: At the historic Santa Monica Pier are Beetles from two eras: a silver 1998 New Beetle from Volkswagen North America and Nicholas Cardin's beautiful red 1964 Beetle. *Matt Stone, courtesy* Motor Trend *magazine*

On the back cover: This 1995 GTI VR6 came with a 172-horsepower narrow-angle V-6. It transformed the standard Golf into one of the best pocket rockets ever built.

Designed by Rebecca Allen

Printed in the United States of America

Contents

Acknowledgments 4

Introduction   **From People's Car to the New Beetle** 5

Chapter 1   **Beetle Sedan 1946–1952** 12

Chapter 2   **Beetle Sedan 1953–1957** 21

Chapter 3   **Beetle Sedan 1958–1964** 24

Chapter 4   **Beetle Sedan 1965–1977** 28

Chapter 5   **Super Beetle 1971–1976** 34

Chapter 6   **Beetle Convertible 1946–1979** 41

Chapter 7   **Karmann-Ghia 1955–1973** .47

Chapter 8   **Special-Bodied Type 1 Cars 1949–1968** 54

Chapter 9   **Transporter, Kombi, Microbus,**
           Vanagon, & EuroVan 1950–1999 58

Chapter 10   **Kübelwagen, Schwimmwagen, and The Thing 1941–1975** . .68

Chapter 11   **Type 3 1961–1973** 73

Chapter 12   **Type 4 1968–1974** 78

Chapter 13   **K70 1970, Dasher (Passat) 1973–1981, and Fox 1987–1994** . .81

Chapter 14   **Golf/Rabbit 1974–1984** 84

Chapter 15   **Polo 1975–1999** 94

Chapter 16   **Scirocco 1974–1988** 97

Chapter 17   **Syncro, Quantum, Vanagon and Golf 1986–1989** 106

Chapter 18   **Quantum 1982–1988** 112

Chapter 19   **Jetta 1980–1992** 116

Chapter 20   **Golf 1985–1992** 122

Chapter 21   **Corrado 1990–1995** 128

Chapter 22   **Passat 1989–1997** 133

Chapter 23   **Jetta III 1993–1999** 141

Chapter 24   **Golf III 1993–1999** 147

Chapter 25   **Passat 1998–1999** 159

Chapter 26   **New Beetle 1998–1999** 163

Chapter 27   **Around the Bend** 170

                Index 176

Acknowledgments

In the five years since the first edition of the *Illustrated Volkswagen Buyer's Guide* was published, Volkswagen has unveiled a new line of cars, exciting new engines, and the remarkable New Beetle. Thus we have updated the appropriate chapters to reflect all the new models as the famous German automaker approaches the new century.

Working with Volkswagen United States, Inc., has been a pleasant experience. We wish to thank Jonathan Mobily and Tony Fouladpour of Volkswagen Public Relations for providing us with hundreds of photos and specifications. A special thanks must go to Volkswagen enthusiast Zack Miller of MBI Publishing Company, for his patience and assistance, and for making this second edition of the *Illustrated Volkswagen Buyer's Guide* possible.

Finally, it would be remiss if we failed to acknowledge the recent death of Ferry Porsche (1909–1998), whose family not only started this saga but continues to have a significant impact on the fortunes of both Porsche and Volkswagen.

From People's Car to the New Beetle

The story of Volkswagen is one of marvelous cars, pioneering designers, daring leaders, international battles won and lost, some tremendous successes, and some significant failures. What began as a single-model philosophy grew into a multitude of confusing lines, models, and nomenclature. What began as a desire to build an inexpensive car for the masses matured into the act of building some of the finest grand touring (GT) performance cars in the world, on a level with those from Daimler-Benz and BMW. What was once a total denial of competition activity was replaced with factory-encouraged formula.

Volkswagen has indeed come a long way, and some of the latest "Autobahn-burners" will no doubt become classics in the future. The Type 1 Beetle must already be acknowledged as a current, postwar classic. Type 1-based cars constitute almost 50 percent of this guide, and the prewar "Führerwagen," indeed, made Volkswagen what it is today.

Volkswagen as a Postwar Classic

Consider this: The VW Beetle is the most important car in the last half of the twentieth century. From 1950 to 1970, the VW heralded a revolution not in design, but in thought, paving the way for the Japanese invasion of the automotive world. Almost single-handedly, the VW turned around the largest and most lucrative market in the world, that of the United States. Its success gave birth to the Falcon, the Corvair, the Valiant, and a host of other would-be competitors throughout the years.

Ferdinand Porsche's car for the masses. From humble beginnings in 1936 to the latest Corrado VR6, VW has indeed come a long way.

Since 1966, VW's semi-official competition arm, VW Motorsports, has been involved in Formula racing and rallying. Here, Sascha Maaben campaigns the 1992 VW-Rait Formula 3.

The VW Beetle continues to be produced, albeit in Mexico, establishing a production record that far exceeds even that of Henry Ford's immortal Model T. Its reliability, serviceability, and roadworthiness, not to mention charm, convinced millions of Americans that gas-conserving, efficient, small foreign cars were not only a viable alternative to Detroit's wishes, but indeed the way of the future.

VW succeeded where no others did. Although its dominance was occasionally threatened in those heady days of 1957–1968, no other manufacturer even came close to the consistent sales record achieved by VW in America. Now, those contenders are all gone, having either left America's shores or disappeared entirely. The list of manufacturers defeated in their goal to win the hearts of Americans is long: Renault, Simca, Austin, and Fiat, to name but a few. If it wasn't said, it should have been: Conquer the American market, and you conquer the world.

Ironically, with a road map provided by VW, only the Japanese succeeded in this lofty goal. But of the many European small sedans that inundated the United States in the 1950s and 1960s, only VW has survived to the early 1990s, a legacy of its long-term staying power and legendary emphasis on quality, innovation, and outstanding dealer reputation.

The VW Beetle is one of the few bona fide postwar landmark cars still available and restorable at reasonable prices, owing in part to the millions sold, the model's reusable ruggedness, and an ample supply of parts, both original and remanufactured. Although the number of pre-1966 cars is dwindling rapidly, it is higher than that for typical postwar classics. Early VWs are easy—but often misleading—marks for home do-it-yourself restorations, which, with a great deal of patience, can be as good as professional jobs at $50 per hour. And, because many young people today still buy a Beetle as their first car, a nostalgia market for the cars may exist for years to come.

Millions of VWs have been turned into beach buggies, airplanes, golf-course lawn mowers, fiberglass replicars, and customized specials, for the VW was every person's car. Owing simply to the relatively complex electronics required in even the most basic cars today, the world will probably never again see the likes of a VW. In the manner made popular by the Model T, VW parts, engines, transaxles, chassis, and bodies were transformed by millions of active imaginations and artful hands. The Beetle served as the last tool of a waning industrial revolution, to be remembered only by those who restore and enjoy old cars. The mechanical propensities of the VW Beetle, its unique chameleonlike ability to become all things to all people, while decimating its numbers, served to spread the word and its reputation to all corners of the earth.

These unique characteristics also created a cult car, and the Beetle in particular has been almost neglected in postwar classic thought because of this. It is almost as if the Beetle were not a car at all, but a cult symbol, not qualified to take its rightful place in the heavens of the so-called classic car, despite grudging recognition from the experts.

It was sought after, not as the collector item it is, but as the cult car it remains. The large number that remain in roadworthy condition has hampered its status as well. One will see a 1960s-vintage VW in general use almost every day in the United States.

In England, the VW is just attaining cult status, but the problem is the same. "They are still so common in everyday use that the 'Classic' people don't always recognize them, and the owners also set themselves apart, feeling that they know something everyone else doesn't!" wrote Robin Allen, a British Beetle

VW's success has long been compared to that of the immortal Ford Model T. The 20 millionth Beetle stands next to Henry's T, of which 15,007,033 were produced.

America was captivated by the Beetle, and so was Disney Studios. The Herbie movies were perhaps the most popular automotive films ever made.

American college students took to the Beetle as well. "Car-stuffing" contests often featured the Volkswagen. VW had truly conquered the American market.

owner. Hopefully, this book will encourage the "coming out" of the VW—not only the Beetle, but the later worthy additions, rear engined and front engined, designed and produced by the VW factory in Wolfsburg, Germany.

Ratings

Always the source of much conjecture, ratings are subjective and, at best, good guesstimates. They are also relative. Ratings are indicators of desirability from the collector's point of view, not of how good a car is.

For a start, we can safely assume that the most collectible VW is the Hebmüller convertible, of which some 696 were built from 1949 to 1952—ergo, five stars. We can also assume, although not quite as safely, that the least desirable VW ever produced was the Dasher—therefore, one star. (It is not a bad car, but is simply low on the list of collectible priorities.) The difficulties begin in the middle. What do we do with the 411/412? It was so disastrous that it has become a German Edsel, and I wouldn't be at all surprised to find that its desirability as a collectible increases in a few years.

Ratings indicate collectible status, yet I have included all VWs up to the present time. VW has made this easy by providing enthusiasts with surefire future collectibles, such as the Golf VR6, the Corrado, and the New Beetle.

So, take the rating system in stride. I, too, am prone to utter a loud "hrummph!" when I read that some automotive writer rates my current possession a few rungs lower than I. There is no such thing as an impartial owner.

The 1980s witnessed the height of old-car prices. The ensuing, and anticipated, fall brought

Dune buggies—most evolving from Bill Devin's original idea—proved the versatility and reliability of the Beetle. Off-road events such as the Baja 1,000 proliferated as the number of dune buggies increased.

many prices back within the grasp of the enthusiast, but also meant the end of speculation. It is difficult to see what the 1990s will bring in terms of automotive investments, but above all, remember that buying any car is rarely the way to make a financial gain, even in the best of times. Although car prices have rolled back, restoration costs have not, negating any serious profit margin, particularly for low-end collector cars such as the VW. The old adage "It costs as much to chrome the bumper of a Ford as of a Ferrari" rings true here. Trying to convince your better half that the VW you want is a good investment may not be very convincing. When in the market for any type of vehicle, buy what you desire, not what you think you can profit from.

Trying to anticipate what may become sought after in a few years is also difficult. A few good bets are out there: Pre-1966 VWs have continued to increase in rarity and therefore in price. A convertible of any type or year is almost always a better bet than a sedan, as are special-bodied cars or factory oddballs and one-offs. Fully equipped vans will almost always bring more than the odd Transporter. But the market is always fickle and unpredictable, and often shows astonishingly poor automotive judgment—witness the Edsel phenomenon. Those who know too much are often lousy soothsayers.

However, a good part of our job is to try to determine what ratings—subjective values that are not necessarily related to investment potential—to apply to older, well-established VWs and to the modern-era front-drive cars as well. Even the old ones can be tough. A well-restored or mint original Type 3, at its best a rustic Wolfsburg loser, may well fetch more than a Beetle of a similar year and condition.

Newer ones are tough as well. Some appear to be logical contenders for collectible status, such as the early Sciroccos and most certainly the Rabbit GTIs.

The Beetle was a servant to all; engines were used in airplanes, chassis were clothed with special bodies, and many hybrids were used on the farm.

Star code	Rating	Supply	Demand
★★★★★	Excellent	Very limited	Highest
★★★★	Very good	Below average	High
★★★	Good	Average	Above average
★★	Fair	Above average	Average
★	Poor	High	Low

Beetles in the water. Malc Buchanan made the run between the Isle of Man and the English coast in a slightly modified Beetle. The Beetle's "floatability" also saved lives on a number of occasions

For more than four decades, the Beetle made its mark in every possible way. It was a difficult act to follow, but VW is looking forward to the twenty-first century with new and exciting models.

Remember your first Beetle? The New Beetle with its unique and unmistakable shape has captured the hearts of both young and old alike. No car since the 1961 Jaguar XKE has generated so much showroom excitement.

On the other hand, first-year pea green Rabbits might skyrocket simply because they were the first VWs to break quite abruptly from the past. Or perhaps the Westmoreland Rabbits, once roundly disapproved of, will gain stature because they were made in the good ol' United States, a production anomaly that lasted less than 10 years.

Thus, without a crystal ball, I can only offer general guidelines, based on hunches provided by experience garnered through years of guesswork.

For those who desire a practical future collectible that can be driven daily and found at a record low price, that mint early Rabbit may be just the ticket. A show winner today might take the shape of an early VW camper, complete with birch wood trim, 1950s-era sink, and vented front windows. For others, owning a VW might mean re-creating a love van straight from the days of Haight-Ashbury, or a tinted-window low-rider customized sedan. An early Sciroc-co may provide fun and performance with a classic flair, and slipping behind the wheel of the latest Corrado will please even the most discriminating buyers. When dealing with VWs, the variety is endless, mak-ing the desire to own one a versatile and enjoyable car madness.

Nearing the end of the century, Volkswagen continues to offer affordable European quality cars as viable alternatives to Japanese and American automakers. Constant improvements in safety, comfort, and reliability have made new models from Volkswagen second to none in their respective price categories. Sales, at a low in 1993, have climbed each year. VW of America has simplified its product line and embarked on a new and effective marketing campaign, and introduction of the New Beetle (an American market initiative) promises to attract new and old buyers alike. The attractive new Passat range offers room and style, and the Golf/Jetta is now targeting Generation X with limited edition models like the Trek and K2. For the enthusiasts, the Golf VR6 brings back the thrill of the original Golf GTI with outstanding performance. The heritage of service and engineering continues, and the new models will ensure that VW will be a force to be reckoned with as the new millennium approaches.

Chapter 1

Beetle Sedan 1946–1952

Historically, the 1946–1952 Beetle sedan is the most important VW ever produced. The first-production VW was the product that symbolized the German economic miracle. It was the fruit of Ferdinand Porsche's long labors, the result of Adolf Hitler's dream, and a prime example of one society's efforts to rise above the ashes of wartime ruin.

Porsche's design, although radical during the mid-1930s, incorporated ideas from a number of sources, including those of engineer Hans Ledwinka, of the Czechoslovakian automobile firm Tatra, and aerodynamics pioneer Edmund Rumpler. Hitler himself provided certain insights, and the entire concept of a German *Volkswagen* (people's car) is generally accredited to a Jewish visionary by the name of Josef Ganz. The name Volkswagen was a generic term until copyrighted by VW after World War II. Prior to the war, the VW was known as the KdF *(Kraft durch Freude*, Strength through Joy) after a Nazi recreational organization. The final Porsche prototype, the Type 38 KdF-Wagen, so familiar to us now, was a blend of ideas from a variety of people, most of whom were not born in Germany.

Prior to the start of World War II, and before the factory at Wolfsburg was constructed in 1938–1939, a total of 124 KdF-Wagens were built at the Daimler-Benz factory, used for durability testing, and sold to Nazi officials. During the war, the new factory concentrated on producing the military Kübelwagen, Schwimmwagen, and Type 51. It was not until 1945, when the British Army took control of the factory, that production of the Volkswagen truly commenced.

A short history of the evolution of the Beetle: Ferdinand Porsche's 1932 prototype built for Zündapp in 1932 featured a 1,200-cc five-cylinder radial engine mounted behind the rear axle.

What rolled out of the rubble and water of World War II—elements that hindered production for years—was a continuation of Porsche's Type 38 and Type 39. During the war, their original 986 cubic centimeters (cc) was increased to 1,131 cc to meet German Army specifications. The new managers called the chassis the Type 1, and to be more specific, the Type 11 designated the sedan, the Type 13 the sunroof model, the Type 14 the two-seat convertible, and the Type 15 the four-seat convertible.

The first cars were stark machines. Little or no brightwork was available, and no metal strip was used along the running boards. Hubcaps, bumpers, and overriders were painted. Seats were cloth, and steering wheels were spindly three-spoke items with a center horn button. Gloveboxes on either side of the painted metal dashboard were open, and a "backward" 120-kilometer/hour speedometer was placed in the center; early speedometers bore the VW emblem at the top. Directly above was placed the lever used to operate the solenoid-controlled signal semaphores. One plastic sun visor adorned the driver's side, and an interior light was placed between the two sides of the split rear window. No headliner material was installed around the rear windows. Notable was the lack of vent windows in the doors, and door panels were plain cloth without pockets. An 8-gallon fuel tank incorporated a 1-gallon reserve tank, which

Ferdinand Porsche's son Ferry sits behind the wheel of the 1935 prototype. The Beetle was beginning to take shape.

could be opened by a lever. The cars had no gas gauge.

The gearshift was embossed with what is now referred to as the KdF symbol—a VW emblem surrounded by gear teeth—which was a leftover from the war years. This famous emblem was created in 1937 by engine designer Francis Xaver Reimspiess of Porsche, who received 100 reichsmarks for his effort. Also unique to the early cars was a small indentation in the roof just above the windshield, which served as an antenna mounting platform and was used on all VWs until October 1952. Brass identification tags

1945 Type 1 Sedan Specifications

Wheelbase	94.5 in
Track, front and rear	50.8 in and 49.2 in
Tire size	4.5x16 or 5x16
Chassis	Steel platform, central backbone, front torsion bar suspension, rear independent suspension with transverse torsion bar
Steering	Worm and roller
Engine	Air-cooled alloy flat-four, thermostatically controlled fan, oil cooler with gear pump pressure lubrication, 6-volt electrical system
Displacement	1,131 cc
Bore x stroke	75x64 mm
Horsepower	25 hp at 3,600 rpm
Compression ratio	5.8:1
Transmission	Four-speed, nonsynchromesh
Brakes	Four-wheel mechanical
Performance	0–30 mph in 9.7 seconds, 0–40 mph in 14.1 seconds, 0–60 mph in 37.2 seconds, top speed of 66 mph
Production	1,785 units

By 1937, the sedan was ready. Porsche had adopted a flat four-cylinder engine configuration. It makes you wonder what happened to the larger window area featured on the 1932 Zündapp design.

One of the prototypes built by Daimler-Benz. Porsche's small car was part of Hitler's agenda to modernize and mobilize Germany.

were found behind the spare tire and included the chassis number, weights, and manufacturer's date. Just below, stamped into the metal of the body itself, was a body number.

Mechanically, the 25-horsepower cars had a Solex carburetor sans accelerator pump, and the VW emblem was embossed on the float bowl, topped by a small round air cleaner. A starting crank was provided, and the access hole was located under the engine lid through the back plate. These cars were not fast—which was a plus, considering the mechanical brakes. They were, however, light, nimble, and sensitive, and a lot of fun to drive.

Such was the basic Beetle.

1946–1948

By the end of 1946, a whopping 10,200 VWs had been produced and sold, primarily to occupation

Thirty prototypes were built and used for testing in 1937, and all seemed to have even less window area. Tests improved the engine and torsion bar reliability.

forces, as quickly as they could be made. Few changes were made; VW did not incorporate "model year" changes until 1955. Brakes were improved, and 5x16-inch tires were standardized.

In 1947, another 8,989 VWs were manufactured, again with few changes, save that hubcaps had a larger VW emblem.

The year 1948 brought significant changes to VW. First, on January 2, 49-year-old Heinz Nordhoff assumed total control of the factory. Second, the implementation of the Marshall Plan transformed the German economy. Although Nordhoff claimed he did not directly benefit, the plan meant suppliers' products increased not only in number, but in quality. Then, on June 20, the old German reichsmark was replaced by the deutsche mark, and citizens once again had a viable, stable currency.

Under Nordhoff's sure hand, production increased, while he sought to both improve quality and reduce the number of hours needed to manufacture one car, from 300 to 100. Production totaled 19,244 units, and few if any changes were made to the car. Again, most examples were sold to occupation forces, which was another thing Nordhoff sought to change. With the new currency, as well as the efforts of Dr. Karl Feuereissen, who managed the sales, distribution, and parts network for VW, Germans now started buying the car Hitler had promised them 10 years earlier.

1949: Chassis Numbers 91,922 to 138,554

Heinz Nordhoff had decided to stay with the basic design—a startling choice when yearly face-lifts and planned obsolescence were gaining popularity among U.S. automakers. "Offering people an honest

The people's car design was finalized by 1938, and aside from the engine displacement, few other major changes were made until 1958. Note the split rear window, glass-covered headlights, and hood. At the car's selling price, little money was available for chrome bumpers

value . . . appealed to me more than being driven around by a bunch of hysterical stylists trying to sell people something they really don't want to have," said Nordhoff, who managed to keep this philosophy until his untimely death in 1968. If the VW was Porsche's baby, then it was even more Nordhoff's child. The Beetle reflected the personality of Nordhoff as surely as it did those of its originators.

In 1949, a Deluxe (surely an optimistic use of the word) version of the Beetle was available. Standard models continued the use of an external hood latch handle, while the Deluxe had an inside release. More brightwork was making a welcome appearance, including a chrome—but still external—horn placed behind the bumper on the standard models and behind the fender on the Deluxe version. Hubcaps were chrome, and the large VW emblems introduced in 1948 gave way to smaller logos. Solex carburetors were standardized with a mushroom-shaped air filter. The rearview mirror was a distinct oval, and the instrument panel, the steering wheel, and most knobs were black. In an optimistic mood, the starting handle, along with its hole and support on the rear

bumper, disappeared during the year—features never given up by arch rivals Renault 4CV and Dauphine. Nordhoff's "fellow employees" more than doubled their 1948 run, totaling 46,146 cars for the year.

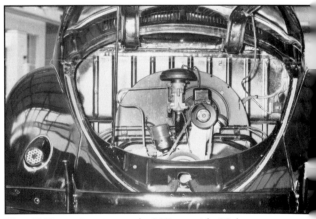

The 1938 engine was only 985 cc with 23 horsepower. The displacement was raised to 1,131 cc during World War II. The war stopped true production of the people's car.

The dashboard of the 1938 car remained largely unchanged until 1952. The speedometer appeared to be upside-down, and the shift pattern was illustrated in a large circle to the right of the speedometer.

1950: Chassis Numbers 138,555 to 220,471

If Heinz Nordhoff was to continue rolling out such figures—by the end of 1950, another 81,979 cars were made—markets would have to be developed. After initial failures in the United States, Nordhoff was apprehensive. "We will have to make our own way in the world without American dollars," he stated in 1949, after an unsuccessful visit to the Unit-

The luggage compartment of the 1938 prototype. Major changes over the years dealt with the size and design of the gas tank to provide more space.

ed States. However, in 1950, Max Hoffman, a New York dealer instrumental in bringing Porsche, Jaguar, and other European exotics to the United States, decided to take on a few VWs, selling 330 of them.

By the end of 1953, only 2,173 VWs had been sold in the United States, which is why these early cars are so hard to find, in any condition, today. Nevertheless, VW was gearing, and dressing, up to meet a developing market. The Deluxe model offered much-needed hydraulic brakes, a sunroof option, trim on the running boards for the first time, and a VW logo on the hood, to the rear of a chrome hood trim. An aluminum hood handle with inside release was now standard. Chrome strips extended from fender to fender on each side of the Deluxe. The horn, now behind the fenders on all models, was placed on the driver's side behind a circular metal grille. Deluxe cars also featured a two-spoke ivory-colored steering wheel and an assortment of ivory-colored plastic knobs replacing the black. The Deluxe speedometer, still "backward," was now surrounded by a white cluster, and beside it was an optional matching clock. The seats were still cloth, but many had contrasting vinyl piping. The previously oval, inside rearview mirror was now rectangular. The Deluxe version was beginning to look very upmarket.

In addition to the hydraulic brakes, an effective handbrake now operated on the rear wheels. The air cleaner was given yet another look, this time log-like. The spotlight remained as before, combined with the license plate light in the center of the engine lid. Mufflers for the heating ducts, and a heat riser, appeared, and the gas tank capacity increased to 10 gallons. Finally, the fenders were insulated from the body with welting in contrasting color to the body.

Quality and material were improving. Pride in artisanship began to develop, establishing a reputation for German firms that continues to this day.

1951: Chassis Numbers 220,472 to 313,829

Despite all odds, the VW had succeeded. New models, including the Transporter and convertible were already in production, and additional factories were being constructed near a growing Wolfsburg. To commemorate the town, the Wolfsburg crest was mounted up front, just above the hood handle.

Bright trim around the front windshield was added, and vent flaps were installed just forward of the doors to aid interior ventilation (vent windows were still a year away). The taillights shed the chrome ring surround, and door armrests appeared on the passenger-side doors. Passenger-side "grab handles" and flower vases (to be reborn with the New Beetle in 1998), both on the dashboard, and passenger-side sun visors were popular options.

1952: Chassis Numbers 313,830 to 428,156

This production year, which lasted from March 1952 to March 1953, was confusing, and some of the modifications summarized for it did not apply to the entire year.

In 1952, the vent flap was replaced or augmented by side vent panels and vent windows were added. In October 1952, a chrome trim was added to the rear split window of the sedan. Again in

The factory identifies this as a 1948 model. Still with no chrome, it was a basic car with no frills. No vent windows had yet appeared, and KdF symbols still could be found on various parts.

By contrast, the 1949 model appeared almost luxurious. Already, Heinz Nordhoff had his eye on the export market. Note the rectangular mirror, unusual for 1949 models, indicating that this was possibly a late example.

The 1949 export model also boasted an upgraded interior, grab handles, and an interior light. The rear armrest cushions were offered in 1951 on the export model, but seen in Europe as early as 1949.

October, the instrument panel was redesigned to incorporate a speedometer placed on either side of the dash. The split rear window continued until March 1953. Window cranks were improved, and along with the new dash, the signal indicator was placed on the steering column. Brake lights were incorporated into the signal lights.

Tires were a definite change: The 16-inch-diameter version was reduced to 15 inches, and 5.6-inch tires replaced the earlier 5-inch ones. The driver finally got the Porsche-patented synchromesh, at least on the last three gears. A total of 114,338 more VWs entered a world still starving for cars.

A late split-window Deluxe version with the sunroof and all available options would be the best choice of any VW Beetle sedan. Materials had improved significantly by the time these were produced, and hydraulic brakes and the synchromesh transmission were desirable. The split-window retained the prewar charm of the car, faithful to the original Porsche Type 38. Compare a clean Deluxe split-window with a late Super Beetle, and you will see what I mean. However, the Deluxe was down on power—remember, we're still talking only 25 horsepower. The car was *slow*.

An early Beetle may not be practical for everyday transportation, and you may also hesitate to drive one

Two-spoke steering wheels were an export or Deluxe feature in 1950, as was the optional clock, which replaced the prewar shift pattern circle. The center switch controlled the semaphore signal arms.

daily, owing to the cost of either purchase or restoration. Location is also important. I wouldn't drive *any* vehicle every day in New York City or even Washington, D.C., but as an around-town car in Sebring, Florida, a 1946–1952 Beetle might work out nicely.

The 1951 models had chrome trim around the windshield, front vent flaps, and the Wolfsburg crest above the luggage compartment handle. VW now had hydraulic shocks and brakes on all four wheels, for export only.

This view of the 1951 model clearly shows the semaphore indicators and small round taillights. Note the groove in the bumpers, which would disappear in 1953.

In October 1952, the rear window incorporated bright metal trim. The taillights were restyled, with a heart-shaped upper lens, used for the stop function. By 1954, the U.S. export models reverted to a simpler, more oval single lens.

What to watch for? In a word, *rust.* This advice applies to all Beetles, regardless of year, so I will not repeat it. Check battery boxes, sills, suspension attachment points, rear panels, the luggage compartment, and heat exchange boxes. The engines have been replaced by later units on many examples, and the same goes for transmissions—particularly the nonsynchros—and any other parts that may have counterparts that fit from later cars, including hydraulic brakes.

Another area of advice I will dispense with here concerns details. This applies to any purchase but is most critical with the early cars, as parts for these can no longer be found in scrap yards. (Super Beetles are still in the yards in abundance.) Parts are difficult to find, particularly the small, detail items—proper coils, carburetors, air cleaners, fixtures, moldings, chrome trim, interior materials—that make the difference between a superb restoration and an average one. Finding the small items often takes years of patience and

scores of contacts. Although costly, rust repair and paint are the "easy" parts of restoration. Many buyers can be swayed by an impressive paint job (make certain it is the right color) and shiny chrome, ignoring the missing or improper items.

When buying, if you are playing the big dollars for what you assume to be a properly restored car, bring an expert and look for the details as well as the overall condition. One dismaying occurrence—and it happens all too often—is for a first-time buyer to select a car, pay top dollar, bring it to a show, and have it torn to pieces in judging. "Wrong headliner material, wrong instruments, missing rubber molding, missing tool kit, wrong-era radio, nonoperational semaphores"—these are all remarks that might be heard as the hapless once-proud owner is subjected to expert judging. And as the previous owner might now be willing to explain, these are often items that deutsche marks alone cannot buy. Which was probably why the previous owner sold the car in the first place.

Chapter 2

Beetle Sedan 1953–1957

From 1953 to 1957, the last years of the "classic VW," the cars lacked the charm of the split rear window but retained the small front window and the overall attractive simplicity of Porsche's initial design. Yet many more were produced—a total of 1,347,234, versus 376,338 of the split-windows—making these later models less expensive and at the same time easier to restore. For those who are looking for a practical vehicle for which an ample number of parts still exist, yet want the traditional classic lines, the 1953–1957 VW is probably the best value.

That the later cars are far superior automobiles is without question. That they are far more practical, usable, and drivable is also a given. However, increasingly with each year past 1958, they are almost caricatures of the earlier but cleaner cars. From a purely aesthetic perspective, the unadulterated pre-1958 cars win hands down. For many collectors, such differences make the difference. It is, albeit to a lesser degree, the same reason a 1957 Thunderbird is more valuable than the new and "improved" 1958 Thunderbird.

Pre-1958 VW models come with a romantic nostalgia, from what Heinz Nordhoff called the Golden Fifties. Although Nordhoff was not being the least bit sentimental—his statement was made in conjunction with a speech on moving forward—the 1950s were nonetheless golden

The first VW arrives in the United States in January 1949, one of two sold in the United States that year. Ben Pon, left, was given the almost impossible task of marketing the Beetle stateside. Persistence paid off.

Made in der Black Forest by der Elves read a VW bumper sticker in the 1950s. Well, that was not quite true. These photos from the late 1940s show the casting of VW blocks. Postwar manufacturing conditions were appalling.

A worker pulls a newly cast block from the die. Conditions improved rapidly as Heinz Nordhoff poured profits back into the war-torn factory.

for VW. Furthermore, they were golden for the hardy few who had dared to establish dealerships and distributorships in the United States. The story of VW in America is well but not completely told in Walter Henry Nelson's *Small Wonder*, still a landmark VW book.

For VW owners, or owners-to-be, the stories of Johnny von Neumann in California, Bob Fergus in Ohio, Carl Schmidt in Chicago, and many more are an integral part of the VW fascination. Laughed at

and derided at first, the dealers who refused to give up—and followed the "company line"—became, in a very short time, very wealthy indeed. Ironically, in 1953, the man who had first imported the VW, Max Hoffman, was denied a renewal of his contract, an event no doubt he would later regret.

Increasingly, the factory began to prepare standard, or home-market cars, and export versions, as well as the Deluxe models. Roughly 50 percent of the cars were sold in Germany, and the remaining half were exported.

1953: Chassis Numbers 428,157 to 575,414

From March 1953, all VWs incorporated a plain oval rear window, a modest attempt to increase the serious lack of rearward vision. A separate brake master cylinder reservoir was added, placed behind the spare tire, and a lock button was appended to the vent windows.

The most radical visible change since 1938 occurred when VW restyled the rear window in March 1953. Vent windows appeared in late 1952 and were made lockable in 1953. Notice the new dashboard, with the speedometer centered behind the steering wheel.

1954: Chassis Numbers 575,415 to 722,934

The big change for 1954 was an increase in performance, brought about by the addition of 61 cc and 5 more horsepower. Horsepower ratings are confusing; some books quote 25 to 30 horsepower, whereas others cite 30 to 36 horsepower, without regard to Society of Automotive Engineers (SAE) or DIN ratings. DIN numbers, the German ratings, are based on horsepower at the rear wheels, whereas the SAE measured horsepower at the flywheel, which gave a more optimistic reading. Commonly, the original 1,131-cc engine is referred to as the 30-horsepower, and the 1,192-cc engine is referred to as the 36-horsepower model, which later produced 40 horsepower from the same displacement. Most important, however, is the increase, as even one honest horse can make a difference in a small, lightweight car. But what happened in the case of the VW is a good question. As tested in *Road & Track* in 1954, the 5 or 6 additional horsepower netted little gain, and in fact, the 0–60-miles-per-hour time recorded with a 1952 model was 2 seconds faster than the slow 39.2 seconds recorded in 1954.

Significantly, *Road & Track* devoted a large part of the test article describing, quite accurately and almost prophetically, the car's "alarming" oversteering characteristics. Although pleasant and fun for many experienced vintage VW owners, the handling characteristics—which later doomed the Corvair—may take new owners by surprise.

Other changes for 1954 included a key operated ignition switch; the dash-mounted starter button was history. The air filter was changed again with an oil-soaked filter element now installed. U.S. cars, now affected by different lighting regulations, had slightly different taillight lenses.

1955: Chassis Numbers 722,935 to 929,745

The news for 1955 was no more semaphores, at least on U.S. models. New front signal lights were placed low on the front fenders. Tubular overriders were provided front and rear, to give additional protection in parking shunts.

Accessories, both factory and aftermarket, proliferated. One could choose the following items from the factory option list: passenger sun visor; outside front window sun visor; adjustable rearview mirror; two styles of outside mirrors; dash handhold; three choices of flower vases (Rosenthal, tinted glass, and chrome); ivory-colored steering wheel; reading light with mirror; pullout ashtray; cigarette lighter; number plate mount; foglight; curb finder; decorative wheel ring; reclining seats; five colors of floor mats (red, green, brown, blue, and natural); door grip; chrome fender guard; back-up light; national plate; exhaust shield; rear ashtray; rear windows; hanging strap; and coat hook.

The 1953–1954 models were virtually unchanged. New oval taillights and key starting were minor alterations. For 1954, the engine displacement increased to 1,192 cc. The 1955 U.S. models were equipped with front turn signal lights and no longer used semaphore signaling.

Adventures in VW one-upsmanship are plentiful here. Finding mint, VW-produced options to add to your restored Beetle is a rewarding challenge, but no doubt pricey.

1956: Chassis Numbers 929,746 to 1,246,618

In 1956, twin chrome exhaust pipes protruded where once there was one, the tubular overriders became standard on all U.S. cars, and a new steering wheel with an off-center bar replaced the old evenly halved item. Luggage space was increased by virtue of a redesigned fuel tank. Front seatbacks were now adjustable, and the heater knob moved forward on the tunnel. Taillights were moved 2 inches higher on the rear fenders.

1957: Chassis Numbers 1,246,619 to 1,600,439

Tubeless tires were standardized for 1957, and the heater vent was moved within 12 inches of the door, getting the still-marginal heat closer to the driver. Adjustable striker plates and more secure door latches were adapted. The interiors were now almost all vinyl, save the headliner.

★★★
1958–1964
Beetle sedan

Beetle Sedan 1958–1964

It might seem logical to include 1965, the last year of the 1200, in this chapter. However, 1964 was the last year of the old consecutive chassis-numbering system, and the last year of relatively small changes to the glass area.

Furthermore, the seven years from 1958 to 1964 were perhaps the greatest in VW history. During this time, Volkswagen conquered America, inaugurated a trendsetting advertising campaign, developed a worldwide chain of distributors and dealers second to none, and, in the process,

Lemon.

This Volkswagen missed the boat.
   The chrome strip on the glove compartment is blemished and must be replaced. Chances are you wouldn't have noticed it; Inspector Kurt Kroner did.
   There are 3,389 men at our Wolfsburg factory with only one job: to inspect Volkswagens at each stage of production. (3000 Volkswagens are produced daily; there are more inspectors than cars.)
   Every shock absorber is tested (spot checking won't do), every windshield is scanned. Volkswagens have been rejected for surface

scratches barely visible to the eye.
   Final inspection is really something! VW inspectors run each car off the line onto the Funktionsprüfstand (car test stand), tote up 189 check points, gun ahead to the automatic brake stand, and say "no" to one VW out of fifty. This preoccupation with detail means the VW lasts longer and requires less maintenance, by and large, than other cars. (It also means a used VW depreciates less than any other car.)
   Volkswagen plucks the lemons; you get the plums.

Dealer Name

The years 1958-1964 were the Beetle's glory days. What other manufacturer would have dared run this in 1952? Not only were Doyle Dane Bernbach's ads a stroke of genius, but VW of America approved each one.

Although a large rear window made the new 1958 VW easily recognizable, differences in the 1959 and 1960 models were very difficult to spot. External changes were limited to the use of push-button door handles on the 1960 model. This is a standard "home" (European) model, still using the semaphore signaling.

created a legend. For Americans, the 1958–1964 Beetles are perhaps the most loved, best remembered, and the most thoroughly wrapped in nostalgia.

Millions of Americans remember one of these VWs as the car bought by a next-door neighbor, a father, or an uncle, and as the first foreign cars to touch their life. For the first time, a car from overseas gained widespread acceptance in the United States. These years represent the apogee of European car sales in America. Many other manufacturers were to fail on American shores, and a new breed of American car—the compact—would be created to meet the challenge of the imports, of course led by a wide margin by VW.

It was sudden success of the VW that took everyone, save the believers, by surprise. In 1954, a total 8,086 sedans were sold by a patchwork dealership system in the United States. Sales increased to 31,000 in 1955, and in 1957, more than 50,000 units went to eager customers. By 1959, a network of distributors and dealers had been organized by Will van de Kamp, and Doyle Dane Bernbach's advertising magic was in full swing.

This was also the year of the greatest sales of "foreign cars" until the Japanese onslaught of the 1970s. A total 614,131 VWs, MGs Austins, Renaults, and Jaguars came to the States. VW was already far ahead

Another ad from the early 1960s. Simplicity and joy, humor and modesty combined to create a successful ad campaign.

In 1961, the Beetle's engine was uprated to 36 horsepower for export models, but still measured 1,192 cc (it was known as the 1200). This was the last year for the small oval taillights.

of the rest, with 120,442 sedans sold. When the boom came—owing in large part to the unshakable belief in the car held by dealers, distributors, and the factory—VW was ready to meet the demand, not only in numbers of cars but with parts and service. Lack of parts and facilities was a sore spot with Americans that other foreign manufacturers never quite figured out.

Significantly, Japanese cars were virtually unheard of at the time. But the success of VW also laid the groundwork for the entry of Japanese cars into the American market, the results of which are well known. The Japanese took their cue from VW, copied VW's incredible service and parts programs, learned from the advertising that VW made famous, and quickly realized that quality and craftsmanship were key in selling to the Americans.

History and nostalgia aside, these VWs are much more practical than their predecessors and, in fact, can be used as daily classics. Cars and parts are still plentiful; parts are more interchangeable with those of later years; and unless one demands air conditioning or effective heaters, the cars are generally comfortable.

1958: Chassis Numbers 1,600,440 to 2,007,615

A new rear window, now rectangular rather than oval, was the big change for 1958. Not as noticeable was an increase in size for the front windshield, squaring off the earlier contours of the roof. Signal lights were moved to the top of the front fenders, and chrome oval horn screens were now used. Only one

of these screens actually hid a horn; the other was a dummy, and a black plate was placed behind it. Inside, the radio grille, which formerly occupied the center of the dash, was moved to the left of the speedometer. Another vestige of prewar days, the roller accelerator, was replaced by a standard flat pedal. The rear brake size increased.

1959: Chassis Numbers 2,007,616 to 2,528,667

Few surprises occurred in 1959. VW's stubborn resistance to change was being hailed by Doyle Dane Bernbach and widely acclaimed by many inside and outside the industry. Stronger clutch springs, an improved cooling fan belt, and a reinforced frame were the only modifications.

1960: Chassis Numbers 2,528,668 to 3,192,506

The standard VW—rarely seen stateside—continued alongside the Deluxe models, which were the only offering in the Land of Liberty. Steering wheels for 1960 were again redesigned, this time with a dish and horn ring, a safety feature. The old three-spoke wheel of prewar vintage was still in use on standard VWs, but now ivory-colored. The old pullout door handles were replaced with buttons and fixed handles. Inside, the sun visors were padded vinyl, and the seats were redesigned with more comfortable contours. Mechanically, a steering damper and a front antisway bar were added to aid the handling, and the generator output was increased.

1961: Chassis Numbers 3,192,507 to 4,010,994

Improved highways demanded more horsepower by 1961. VW added another 4 horsepower, and the new Beetle owner had a full 40 horsepower pushing self and car—and this time, the difference was noticeable. Shifting was easier now, with synchromesh on all forward gears. A new gas tank shape made room for more luggage, and the brake reservoir was made transparent. Electrically, these cars were still getting along with only 6 volts, but new push-on connectors were adopted, as well as a nonrepeat starter switch. The choke became automatic, and the windshield washer was modified to a pump type.

1962: Chassis Numbers 4,010,995 to 4,846,835

Finally, in 1962, a gas gauge. The old reserve switch was charming, but definitely had its drawbacks. Even a VW could only go but so far on one gallon of gas. VWs rarely won gas mileage contests; their average was only about 25 miles per gallon. A new spring-loaded hood prevented the gas station attendant from creasing, or breaking, the hood at the left-hand stay; checking of pre-1962 VWs will inevitably uncover a brace and weld at this point, repairing damage to the hood, which had been a victim of the careless. Taillights were larger and immediately noticeable. Seatbelt mounts were provided, and the heater vents had a sliding cover. Windshield washers were changed again, this time being pressurized by air from the spare tire. The worm and sector steering box became a worm and roller unit.

1963: Chassis Numbers 4,846,836 to 5,677,118

In late 1962, a perforated vinyl headliner replaced the old cloth one, and the famous Wolfsburg emblem on the hood was dropped; VWs were now being made elsewhere in Germany and in Brazil. Foam was added to the floorboards, the window guides were made of nylon, and fresh air heating was introduced.

The public was beginning to think VW was serious; it would never really change. And why should it? Germany alone produced 747,143 sedans that year, and the demand still was greater than the supply.

1964: Chassis Numbers 5,677,119 to 6,502,399

The traditional vinyl sunroof disappeared in 1964, and although the new steel sunroof was more weatherproof, the opening was about half the size. Inside, the upholstery now echoed the headliner, with perforations for better breathing. The VW emblems on the wheel covers were no longer painted, but a new variety of exterior colors were added: Panama Beige, Java Green (dark), Bahama Blue (light), and Sea Blue. Former colors still available included Black, Pearl White, Anthracite, and Ruby Red.

Changes were afoot, despite the ad campaigns. A new type of VW was being readied for introduction, for even Heinz Nordhoff realized that the VW Beetle could not go on forever. Still, in his wildest dreams, he could not have imagined that the car that had no hope in 1948 would still be in production in 1993.

The 1962 Beetle had larger taillights. The large plastic tube from the air cleaner to the oil filter is the positive crankcase ventilation (PCV) system, the first of many emission control devices to come.

Chapter 4

Beetle Sedan 1965–1977

Post-1964 Beetles have a lot in common, which is of great interest to the potential buyer. They are numerous and still driven daily, and still provide low-cost, low-maintenance transportation. What they lost in charm, they gained in practicality, performance, and safety. The fun factor—that subjective sum of all elements, including parts performance, rarity, cost, reliability, and so forth—may be higher on these models than on any other. Eventually, the last of the Beetles will become collector items, although right now, they are simply too numerous to consider collectible.

The Type 3, known to Americans as the squareback and fastback, was introduced to Europe in 1961 and to the United States in 1966, as the promised replacement. However, the continued market for the Beetles—although not what it was—remained strong, and to sustain it in place of anything else, year by year, the factory continued to make improvements. Many modifications were made as a result of increased safety and emission requirements in the United States. Some "improvements" were simply tacked on, while others, such as air conditioning, overburdened the already taxed powerplant. If the changes in the VW profile seem insignificant when viewed alone, place a 1977 Beetle next to a 1953 model to see quickly what was lost in the name of gains.

Expansion was still under way by means of new factories in Brazil and Mexico. By the mid-1960s, VWs were also produced in Australia and South Africa. In 1993, the Beetle was still produced in Mexico, al-

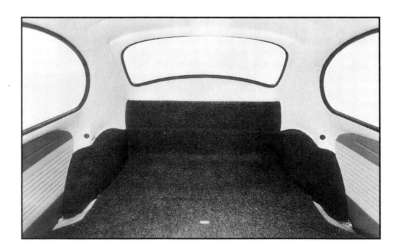

The luggage capacity was increased by the introduction of a fold-down rear seat in 1965. The rear windows also increased in size.

More window area was a much-needed improvement for 1965. Larger windshield wipers parked on the driver's side versus the passenger's side.

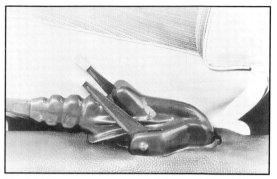

For 1965, new heater control levers allowed heat to enter either the front or rear passenger areas. The famous control knobs were gone.

though it was not legal stateside. The last German Beetle, a white sedan, rolled off the line on January 19, 1978. After that date, all new Beetles sold in Europe were manufactured in Mexico and Brazil.

Slight confusion may arise about 1970–1977 Beetles. As new Super Beetles, they were offered alongside what can now be called the Standard Deluxe. The 1971–1976 Super Beetle, covered in Chapter 5, sold so well that it quickly overshadowed the standard model, which was still available.

The 100 Series VWs, or Type 1s, were the Beetles and Karmann-Ghias. The 200 Series, or Type 2s, cov-

ered the Transporters, Microbuses, and station wagons. The 300 Series, or Type 3s, indicated the VW 1600s. Before 1965, the Type 1s were given numeric chassis numbers. In 1965, a new chassis numbering system was devised. The Beetles, still Type 1s, started fresh with the number 11, for series 1; followed by a 5, for the last number of the year, 1965; and then followed by six digits that counted the chassis, starting with 0 every year. The last 1965 VW in model year 1965 was chassis number 11-5979202, indicating that 979,202 beetles were produced. The chassis numbers for all 1200, 1300, and 1500 cars can be found under the

The What Can We Improve on Next game was in full swing in 1965. The larger windshield was also slightly curved, a push button replaced the turning engine-lid handle, and front turn lights were enlarged. The VW was becoming a "thoughtful" design.

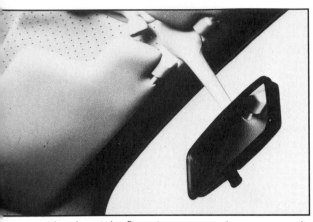

The day-night flip mirror was an improvement in the 1969 model year and included in the Karmann-Ghia coupes. Note the padded visors and perforated headliner material.

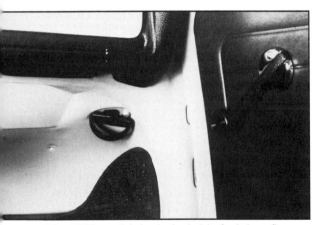

The 1969 models had a lockable fuel door flap, released from the inside. The handle was located near the lower right-hand corner of the glovebox.

back seat on the frame tunnel, and behind the spare.

1965: Chassis Numbers
115-5000001 to 115-5979202

The year 1965 was the year of the big windows—although more was to come. The front windows were slightly curved, with an 11 percent glass increase. The front door glass gained 6 percent; the side quarter windows grew a whopping 17 percent; and the rear window was increased again, this time by 19 percent. The door pillars were thinner to accommodate the increase. The windshield wipers were larger and parked left instead of right; the T-handle

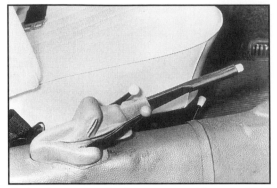

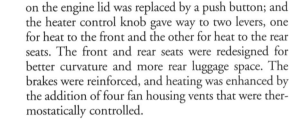

Slight changes to the heater control boot in 1966 probably meant less cracking and tearing.

on the engine lid was replaced by a push button; and the heater control knob gave way to two levers, one for heat to the front and the other for heat to the rear seats. The front and rear seats were redesigned for better curvature and more rear luggage space. The brakes were reinforced, and heating was enhanced by the addition of four fan housing vents that were thermostatically controlled.

1966: Chassis Numbers
116-000001 to 116-1021298

After 12 years, the VW engine displacement was upped to 1,300 cc, or 1,285 cc to be precise, in 1966, and power was increased to 50 horsepower. The old-style wheels and hubcaps were gone, replaced by slotted wheels with a more conventional bolt pattern and flatter hubcaps, usually surrounded by slotted chrome wheel trim. The headlight dimmer was moved from the floor to the signal switch, and a four-way emergency blinker switch was added for the feds. A "1300" script was added to the engine lid.

The performance was now at least ample: *Road & Track* tested a $1,900 1300, for a top speed of 75 miles per hour and 0–60 miles per hour in 25.5 seconds. The magazine staff also figured that despite its faults—it was getting long in the tooth even then—the Beetle "would continue to hold its position of eminence in the economy car field."

1967: Chassis Number
117-7000001 to 117-7844044092

The 1300 was short-lived in the United States; 1967 brought the Beetle 3 more horses from another displacement increase, this one to 1,493 cc, rounded off to 1,500 cc. The 1300 was continued in other countries. Also significant was the change, at long last, to a 12V electrical system. The Volkswagen name replaced the 1300 script, and the lid itself was redesigned for a more vertical placement of the license plate. Back-up lights were now standard. This was the first year of the noncovered sealed-beam headlights. Dual master cylinders augmented the brake system. Discs were available only on the non-U.S. 1,500-cc—a strange decision. Drum brakes would be the only type available in the United States for all years.

1968: Chassis Numbers 118-000001 to 118-1016098

The now familiar one-piece bumpers, headrests, and collapsible steering column were all part of the new safety features in 1968. New rear lights incorporated the back-up lights. Emission controls were mandatory on engines sold in the United States, and the gas filler was now covered by an external opening behind the right front fender. A fresh air intake vent was part of the hood, and the hood was opened with a new push button in the handle. Also, the automatic stick shift was available as an option; it was troublesome, so watch out. Along with that came double-jointed rear suspension, a much more satisfactory way of dealing with independent rear suspension. Push buttons were no longer used on the door handles; a trigger behind the handle now did the trick.

Doyle Dane Bernbach was still at it in 1970–1971. Here, the text of an ad explains that a 1956 VW "is worth more today than any American sedan built the same year with the possible exception of a Cadillac."

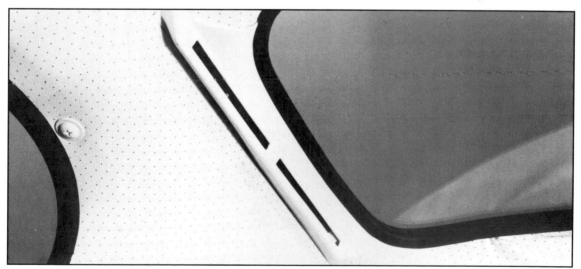

Flow-through ventilation was new to the 1971 model year, as can be seen from the exit vents placed on either side of the rear window.

1969: Chassis Numbers
119-9000001 to 119-91093704

Production was increasing, but 1969 was one of the last good years for numbers. A rear window defroster was wired into the glass, an ignition steering wheel lock was installed, a day-night rearview mirror was opened with a lever under the right side of the dash. The hood release was hidden in the glovebox.

1970: Chassis Numbers
110-02000001 to 110-03096945

A new speedometer read in tenths of a mile; vehicle identification numbers were mounted on the left front of the dash and were visible through the windshield;

side reflectors were used on the rear taillights and the enlarged front signal lights; and two extra intake vents were added to the engine lid. A new, 1,569-cc engine, called the 1600, meant horsepower was up from 53 to 57.

1971: Chassis Numbers
111-12000001 to 111-13143118

Concentrating on the new Super Beetle, VW did little to the 1971 models aside from adding a flow-through-ventilation air system, which was identified by a small vent just to the rear of the quarter windows.

1972: Chassis Number
112-22000001 to 112-23143118

A four-spoke safety steering wheel, a larger rear

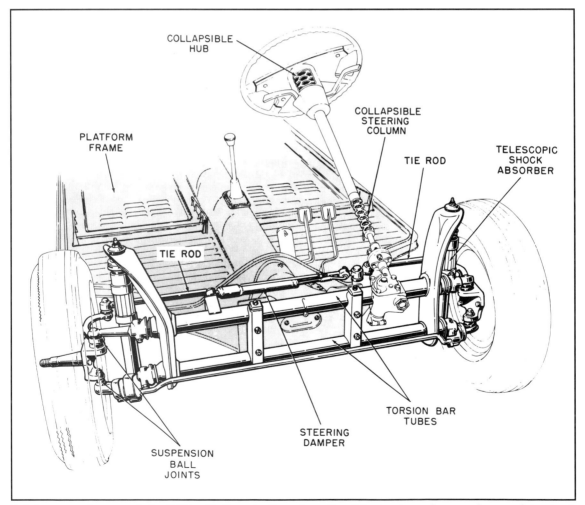

Safety was on the agenda for 1972, with the adoption of a collapsible steering column and new safety wheel.

The end of an era: the last Beetle produced in Germany, at the Emden plant, on January 19, 1978.

window, and a series of four horizontal intake vents were visual changes in 1972. A new diagnostics socket aided troubleshooting—at least for the dealer.

1973: Chassis Numbers
113-32000001 to 113-33021954

Still-larger taillights were installed; the clutch was improved; and the heater levers were redesigned, all for 1973.

1974: Chassis Numbers
114-42000001 to 114-42818456

Production was decreasing for the Beetle; by 1974, the new Rabbit had been introduced. Inside, a new handbrake-safety belt light replaced the earlier style, and "self-restoring" bumpers added weight front and rear.

1975: Chassis Numbers
115-52000001 to 115-52267815

Fuel injection was fitted to the 1600 in 1975, and "Fuel Injection" script was added to the engine lid. No longer in use was the traditional VW emblem on the hood—although the brightwork trim remained. U.S. cars had "Unleaded Fuel Only" stickers on the dash.

1976: Chassis Numbers
116-62000001 to 116-62176287

In 1976, the speedometers were calibrated in both miles per hour and kilometers per hour, and the license plate light fixture was slightly modified.

1977: Chassis Numbers
117-72000001 to 117-72101292

Seats had separate headrests in 1977. A wider range of colors was offered as well, but that was it. This was the last year Beetle sedans were sold in the United States, and the last full year they were made in Germany.

Of course, this is not the end of the story, as the early-style 1200–1600 versions were still being produced in Mexico and sold throughout the world, into the early 1990s. In California, an attempt was made to import the Mexican cars after the demise of the Super Beetle. Called the Peoples Car Company, it apparently sold about 1,500 Mexican Beetles, suitably modified to meet federal regulations, in 1983 and 1984, but further Environmental Protection Agency restrictions made the venture unprofitable. Aside from those few, any Mexican-made Beetles residing in the United States are probably illegal.

Chapter 5

★★
**1971–1976
Super Beetle**

Super Beetle 1971–1976

The Super Beetle was the delayed result of a certain amount of uncertainty at Wolfsburg. By 1968, Heinz Nordhoff was ill, and he had neither chosen a successor for himself nor for the Beetle. The Type 3s were not the answer, as the public had learned. The 411/412 series was a still-more-serious failure, and both had floundered at a time when VW simply had no time to lose. In short, Wolfsburg was caught unprepared for the Japanese onslaught of the 1970s, not to mention the success of U.S. products such as the Pinto and Vega.

Until the production of the new Rabbit was well under way, VW decided to lower the price of the standard VW and introduce an updated model as well. The new Super Beetle, particularly after 1973 when the windshield became wraparound, came off looking like a Beetle after a few rounds with an ungloved Mike Tyson. Swollen, bulging, bulbous, almost preposterous, it hit an increasingly selective market and, almost beyond anyone's expectations, was very successful.

The new cars were tagged the 1302 and 1303 models, or the 1300 and 1600, respectively, when imported to the United States. They were both Type 113s, and their chassis numbers ran 133-20000001 and up.

An improved front suspension in the form of a MacPherson strut-coil spring arrangement provided twice the luggage capacity as that of the standard VW, and a far better turning radius. A slight change was made in the wheelbase, and all Super Beetles had

The underside of the 1971 Super Beetle. Note the now-standard double-jointed rear suspension. Handling was improved but not up to 1970-era standards.

On VW's most successful failure, the Super Beetle, the old Porsche-designed front torsion bar suspension was replaced with MacPherson struts. Also seen here is the new safety steering column.

The fabulous Sports Bug was yellow with black stripes and trim. It was the first of many such special Beetles, most of which came out of Mexico and Brazil.

Left
Use of MacPherson struts allowed the luggage compartment to be almost twice as large as that in the old Bug. Still, the competition offered more.

double-jointed halfshafts. When it came to handling, these cars were a different animal from their predecessors.

Performance was not super, however, since the new Bug weighed in at over 2,300 pounds wet and offered only 46 horsepower, emissions having taken their toll from the previous 50-horsepower models. The 0–60-miles-per-hour dash still took the better part of 18 seconds, and the quarter-mile was run in 21 seconds at 64 miles per hour. The top speed was around 80 miles per hour.

Despite the improvements, the Super Beetle was purely a stopgap, and it showed poorly in the face of

competition. In a *Road & Track* comparison test of five economy sedans, the Super Beetle was in trouble: "No car has ever come in more resoundingly last in a car-to-car evaluation," wrote *Road & Track's* staff. It would have been too much to ask of a prewar design to remain competitive with the latest products from both the United States and Japan. The Super Beetle sold because of the reputation, trust, and reliability garnered by VW since the mid-1950s.

Still priced at under $2,000 port of entry (p.o.e.), the Super Beetle was now available with air conditioning for an additional $267. The semi-automatic was an option at $139. The horsepower ratings varied from 46 to 60, but performance in the various road test of the era gave comparable results, whatever the claimed horsepower. Brakes were still drums, despite the disc brake's being offered in non-U.S. models.

Image was important in the 1970s, and as a result, a number of special models could be ordered. One was called the Sports Bug, and along with the appellation came a three-spoke competition steering wheel, black trim, yellow exterior paint with a black vinyl roof, and Pirelli tires on special wheels. Other special models were available in Europe; with names like Big and City, they offered metallic paint, leather-covered steering wheels, wide wheels and oversized tires, and velvet upholstery.

Super Beetles are readily available for purchase and are in fact still regarded as a good first car for

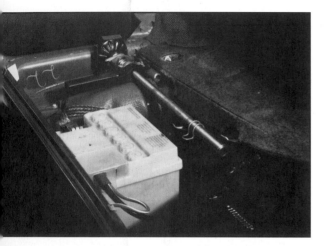

The jack could now be found under the rear seat, along with the battery, and the spare was stored horizontally in front.

Bulbous, what? The 1971 Super Beetle was imported to the United States with the 46-horsepower 1,600-cc engine. Super Beetles are still operating on a reliable, daily basis throughout the United States.

Three inches longer than the standard Beetle, the 1971 Super Beetle was a last-ditch attempt to hold onto what was left of the traditional Beetle market. Roundly criticized, it nonetheless sold amazingly well.

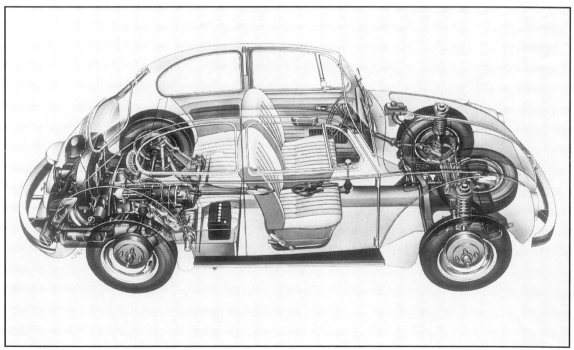

Cutaway of the Super Beetle. Note the four-wheel drum brakes. Discs up front were available in other parts of the globe.

From the rear, the Super Beetle did not appear so heavy, despite the large taillights. This is a 1972 model.

Also noticeable were the very large rear taillights of the 1973 model year. Those too did not fit the overextended body.

Rear view of the 1972 model. The rear window was again enlarged, and the horizontal vents were grouped in four rather than two as in the previous year.

The windshield became wraparound in 1973. Bumpers were still modest. Few other changes were made that year.

The 1973 Super Beetle dashboard. Compare it with the 1938 version. A padded dash and improved ventilation were features in 1973.

Energy-absorbing bumpers and a wider track were two of the improvements for 1974.

many teenagers. If any lessons can be learned from the past, we can be fairly sure that in 10 years, those who choose a used Super Beetle as their first car will have the urge to buy another. That yellow and black Sports Bug may be a good future bet after all.

1971–1972
The year 1971 was the first for the Super Beetle, identified by a small front windshield.

1973–1974
The 1303 in 1973–1974 incorporated a noticeable wraparound front windshield, along with larger taillights. The dashboard was redesigned with more padding, and the internal airflow was improved. In 1974, bumpers became shock absorbing.

1975–1976
For 1975–1976, improvements were made in the rear camber geometry. Rack and pinion steering replaced the worm and roller gears, and the seats were fully reclining.

Overall, the Super Beetle is a hard call. Beloved by its many owners and still in daily use by millions through the early 1990s, it will always have a following. Many examples are being "restored" (a smart move while parts are still plentiful), and asking prices range from the low hundreds to over $5,000. Of all the Beetles, this one is the least desirable, but of all the Beetles, it is also the most practical.

Despite 30 years of constant production and improvements, Super Beetles still tend to rust in the same areas as do 1946 models: sills, the battery area, floors, jacking points, and suspension points. The only smart buy is a rust-free example, so shop around.

Still getting only 25 miles per gallon after all those years, the Beetle was now equipped with every conceivable safety and smog device. It had worn itself out. This 1974 model was nearly identical to the last of the breed in 1975–1976, when the rear camber geometry was changed, rack and pinion steering was introduced, and the seat became fully reclining. Let it rest in peace.

Beetle Convertible 1946–1979

The Convertible story began before World War II, as a special convertible model, nearly identical to postwar versions, was built and used for the ground-breaking ceremonies at Wolfsburg in 1938. The KdF convertible was not to be part of the planned production run, however, despite the intense interest Hermann Goering had in it.

After the war, two special convertibles were constructed for two British officers in charge of the VW plant—Colonel C. R. Radclyffe and Major Ivan Hirst. In 1948, with Heinz Nordhoff now in control, the German Police requested an open version of the Beetle for patrol work. Not having enough facilities at Wolfsburg, the 2,000-car project was farmed out to the Hebmüller firm in Wulfrath, Germany. By 1952, Hebmüller had built only 696 two-seat models, as the plant had suffered a fire in 1949 and never regained full operating capacity. The

Ernst Reuters' beautiful and dramatic artwork highlighted the VW Cabriolet brochures in the 1950s. His paintings made the Beetle seem much more streamlined than it actually was.

A 1955 convertible, probably a home-market model, as it still sports the traditional semaphore signaling.

Hebmüllers are perhaps the most attractive of all special-bodied VWs. (They are covered in Chapter 8.)

Hebmüller's loss was Karmann's gain. Wilhelm Karmann, Sr., began making car bodies in 1901, taking over an even older firm by the name of Klages, located in Osnabrück, Germany. Throughout the 1920s and 1930s, Karmann specialized in convertible bodies for Adler, Minerva, and Opel. In 1948, at the age of 78, he went to Wolfsburg to purchase a Beetle to modify, and came back with an order from Nordhoff for 1,000 four-passenger Convertibles.

The design for the four-passenger Convertible was a near carbon copy of the 1938–1939 prototype, with the bulky top stacked in the rear, allowing rear seat room but reducing rearward visibility. Still, it was one of those designs that was right from the start—and although not as attractive as the Hebmüller, it was more practical.

By 1950, Karmann had filled the first order for 1,000 cars, and the VW factory provided the firm with more orders—a process that would continue until the last Beetle Convertible rolled off the line at

The convertibles incorporated all the changes made to the standard sedan through the years. Note the heavier overriders on this 1957 model.

Osnabrück on January 10, 1980. In those 30 years, Karmann built 331,847 Beetle Convertibles, not a big number by any means. They were known as the Type 15.

Meanwhile, it was reported that Herr Hebmüller was wasting time and money on wine, women, and song, using 100-mark notes to light cigars. Apparently, the hard-working Nordhoff caught wind of Hebmüller's lifestyle and was not impressed. Karmann got the contract to produce the four-place open Beetle, and Hebmüller languished.

Although not unique, VW and Karmann offered what few other postwar manufacturers did: a full, almost luxurious convertible based on an economy car. Convertible sales brochures from 1952 to the early 1960s were beautifully illustrated by Ernst Reuters, who managed to make the ungainly Beetle appear almost sleek and smooth and sexy, albeit in a 1950s manner. The brochures—collector items in themselves—were printed in color on thick, quality paper, and extolled the virtues of the convertible in no uncertain terms.

VW's well-constructed, padded, and weatherproof top meant that its Convertible was versatile and

VW convertibles had a number of popular accessories, such as the chrome rear fender guards and beauty rings seen on the 1960 version.

practical, as early brochures were eager to explain: "In two ways it [The Convertible] really forms two cars in one: open, with fully lowering side pieces, this uncompromising full convertible is a true sporting comrade for nature-loving motorists. Closed, the thickly padded, sound absorbing folding top, with its rear window now enlarged almost by half, offers the same coziness and protection from the dust, wind, and weather

Classic shape, classic design. The 1961 VW, with the Wolfsburg crest still on the hood; low, covered headlights; and nonoffending bumpers.

Not much could be said for rearward version in 1961, or any other year. It was compromised: Designers wanted to retain the rear seat space, rather than bury the top.

The larger taillights of the 1962 model are obvious. The rear window was also enlarged by 33 percent in late 1962.

as the steel roof of the sedan." Indeed, few convertibles then or now have featured such a superb top.

However, what was then a major quality selling point becomes today a major expense and headache. From the wood and metal frames to chrome latches and hooks, restoring a Beetle Convertible is costly and time-consuming. A beetle top consists of hundreds of parts, including rubber moldings, glass windows, chrome window surrounds, padding, top material, framework and wood, and hooks and latches, most of which wear out, rust, rot, or simply disappear. Although ample parts seem to be available for 1965–1979 Convertibles, earlier, fabric convertible tops and materials are not as easy to find.

Rust in the side frame members will do an even more extensive job of separating you from your dollar. Even though these girders were reinforced on the Convertible chassis to retain the rigidity of the chassis sans the top, they are still prone to rust and difficult to repair.

Is restoration worth it? The answer is an unqualified yes, again particularly for the earlier, cleaner models. For some reason, the Beetle Convertible worked, not simply in the physical sense,

but aesthetically as well, another point not often shared by convertible conversions. And any model up to the Super Beetle retains that early charm, since the soft top prevented any undue increase in glass area. Notable here, however, is an 8 percent increase in glass area to the front windshield and a 45 percent increase to the rear in 1957, as well as an increase in top height along with a small increase in side glass area, in 1964–1965.

Changes in the Convertible were nearly identical to the mechanical changes introduced to the sedan, even predating the sedan changes in some instances. Options tended to be more numerous on the Convertibles, since for many years they were regarded as the flagship of the VW fleet and appealed to owners who could afford to spend a little more on their automobile, creating a bit of a paradox.

Was the Convertible marketed as an economy car? Again, the 1955 sales brochure clarifies the point: "Through a particularly fine furnishing that takes the most pampered tastes into consideration, a maximum of traveling comfort and enjoyment is offered. The buyer has a choice of many carefully chosen color combinations. The rich chrome trim and highly polished decorations harmonize with the noble style. Strong, durable, highly polished metal corners protect the rear fenders. Among other things, standard equipment includes a second sun visor before the passenger seat and a chrome handhold over the large, locking glove compartment."

That the Beetle Convertible was not just an economy ragtop was quickly verified by the clientele. According to automotive journalist Jan P. Norbye, as soon as export models became available, Beetle Convertibles quickly found buyers such as Brigitte Bardot, Alain Delon, Pierre Cardin, Yves St. Laurent, and even Fiat's Giovanni Agnelli. Hitler's people's car was going upmarket.

Production figures are useful for buyers; they supply numbers for the supply side of the demand formula. But contradictory production numbers are often derived from various sources. Jan Norbye claimed that, by August 1950, as many as 10,000 Convertibles had been produced. Other production statistics list 364 cars made in 1949, and an additional 2,695 in 1950, and another 3,938 in 1951, for

A minor change for 1962 was the fitting of springs on either side of the luggage compartment lid, replacing the mechanical-type catch.

The horn bar mounted in the spokes distinguished 1964 models from earlier ones that had a half-ring around the steering wheel to operate the horn.

a more realistic total 6,997 by 1951. By 1971, production peaked at 24,317 units.

As with the sedan, few Convertibles were imported before 1955, so those early models will be at a premium. In any condition, one can expect to pay almost double for any pre-1303 Convertible. For the first-time collector or buyer, the later Super Beetle genre may be the place to start; it offers a lot of parts, a good selection, and lower prices, along with the same fun and fresh air as the earlier cars provide.

The 1964 VW convertible was still a clean machine. Covered headlights disappeared in 1967, oval horn grilles in 1968.

The Super Beetle convertible, 1975. Ah well. These were more numerous, less classic, but practical. Watch the rust. Fixing body rot may be worth it on earlier convertibles, but questionable on the Super Beetles.

Chapter 7

Karmann Ghia 1955–1973

Karmann-Ghia is a model name that easily rolls off the tongue, has almost a lyrical sound, and became a world-famous trademark long before the general public knew what it meant.

The name was coined by Dr. Wilhelm Karmann, Jr., shortly before the car went on sale in October 1955, after rejecting Italian names such as Ascona, San Remo, and Corona. But Karmann's suggestion was almost perfect, a distinct blend of German and Latin that at the same time gave credit to both the coachbuilder and the design studio.

The car was as successful as the name, if not more so. From those shaky days in 1955 to the end of the line in July 1974, Karmann's little firm in Osnabrück produced 283,501 coupes and 80,897 convertibles; another 23,577 coupes were made in Brazil. The Karmann-Ghia far surpassed its creator's expectations.

It took awhile, perhaps until the mid-1960s, for the public at large to understand that although Karmann had produced the body under contract for VW, the design honors belonged to a small but prolific Italian firm by the name of Ghia. The person responsible for the specific design remains a mystery. To add to the international flavor of the pretty German-Italian car, it seems that a good deal of credit must go to Chrysler's Virgil Exner, who was designing a series of Chrysler dream cars for Ghia to translate into metal. Ghia's owner, Mario Felice Boano,

Although the 1955 Karmann-Ghia appears identical to the 1972 model, note the low-profile headlights, front bumper, and small grilles of this early model. The first-series taillights were very small and rectangular.

The 1957 convertible had a different front end treatment. Headlights had been raised and the grilles elongated. U.S. versions had stronger bumpers with tubular overriders.

The interior of the 1961 Karmann-Ghia convertible. Padded sun visors and dash and a deep dished steering wheel were token concessions to safety.

probably downsized Exner's "Chrysler D'elegance" to VW dimensions. Both Exner and Boano claimed responsibility for the design.

Although the new Karmann-Ghia, the Type 143, was a world sensation in 1955, deliveries to the United States did not begin until 1956, and only 2,452 were imported that year, at a price of $2,395 p.o.e. New York. Sales grew steadily until 1970, when some 38,000 cars were sold. Advertising was virtually nonexistent until 1961, when Doyle Dane Bernbach began to have fun with the concept of an exotic-looking Italian car with humble VW underpinnings.

Ad copy was both tongue-in-cheek and memorable, and it supported the factory's idea of what the car should be and what it should remain: a quasi-sports car, with no pretensions of power or performance. It was not perceptibly faster than its sedan sibling. In Germany, the Karmann-Ghia was commonly referred to as "Little Liza Miller's sports car," as it was perhaps more suited to young girls

Despite the high beltline and small glass area, the Karmann-Ghia was well-proportioned and pleasant to the eye. Improvements in 1961 were all on the inside: better brakes, levers for heating controls, a faster demister.

than a performance-car enthusiast. Wolfsburg steadfastly maintained that the Karmann-Ghia was not in competition with Porsche, or with anyone else for that matter. In maintaining this moderate-performance image, the Karmann-Ghia cut a

The 1300 (1,285 cc) with 50 horsepower was new for 1966. It meant the Karmann-Ghia was good for 80 miles per hour; it was still Little Liza Miller's sports car.

In 1967–1968, side markers make their appearance. the Karmann-Ghia still had classic lines and was a good buy, but watch for bubbles appearing in the rocker panels. Rust was the prime enemy of the Karmann-Ghia.

Restyled taillights were the key to spotting 1972 and later Karmann-Ghias. They dominated the view but added to safety. Bumpers were now one-piece.

marketing niche for itself with no competition in the marketplace—the only place where VW was allowing the car to compete. Ironically, its lack of power was the car's saving grace.

The Karmann-Ghia begged to be accepted for what it was, not what it could be, and today, collectors abide by the same dictum. It is an attractive, limited-production, hand-built body on a stock VW chassis that was necessarily widened girder to girder.

Karmann-Ghias are perhaps the most preferred old stock out there. Prices are rising and will probably continue to rise for the foreseeable future. But forget matching performance with style. Karmann-Ghias will be most valuable as strictly factory stock items. Save your money for rust repair, since that is where it will be needed most.

In addition to the chassis rust suffered by all VWs, the Karmann-Ghia contributes a unique twist to the rust wars. Remember, these were hand-built cars. That is great, but it meant Karmann had to stitch together many small pieces for steel, as it had no large presses at the time. Each weld is subject to

Safety modifications were accomplished with more ease, and taste, on the Karmann-Ghia than on the Beetle. The 1972 bumpers and signal lights did little to spoil the lines of the car.

From the side, the 1972 model retained its charm. A further change, however, involved the front signal lights, now wraparound.

No change occurred in the 1974 models, but disc brakes were now standard on the 1600 version. It was the end of the line, as Karmann readied itself for a new generation of VWs.

rust on its own accord, if body damage weakens the base primer. Lower-body rot is also pervasive. *Quality* in terms of 1950s and 1960s automotive products is not synonymous with *rustproofing*.

If you haven't seen a Karmann-Ghia lately, check out a good one, preferably an earlier model with the small taillights. Two things become obvious: Karmann-Ghias are much smaller and lower than you might recall, and much prettier than almost any photograph shows. The design, although old, has aged well and contributes to the car's status as a highly collectible VW. The construction (never mind the rust) is solid, smooth, and similar to that of the Borgwards, Porsches, and Mercedes-Benzes of the same era. The much-discussed thud of the doors and high quality of the interior, trim, and controls are pleasing effects that are found lacking in modern vehicles.

Mechanical changes kept pace with the sedan throughout the production run, until the advent of the Super Beetle. The Karmann-Ghia design could not accept the MacPherson front suspension of the 1303. The Ghia did, however, benefit from the revised double-jointed rear axle in 1969, unfortunately only available with the semi-automatic transmission. The rear suspension improvements dramatically changed the car's handling. The semi-automatic, however, is not recommended.

Everyone thought the Beetle never changed, but the Karmann-Ghia suffered far fewer body changes. Aside from minor interior and exterior trim

modifications, the only changes made in appearance were to adjust the size of the taillights, alter the parking lights, and add federally mandated 2.5-miles-per-hour bumpers in 1972. But the manufacturer's philosophy was a true case of "If It Ain't Broke, Don't Fix It." Other "major" changes, by year, were as allows:

1958: Fenders and headlights raised, wider air scoops used in the nose.

1960: Dished steering wheel, steering wheel linkage damper, and optional Saxomat vacuum-operated clutch offered.

1961: 1,192-cc engine installed, top speed increased from 68 miles per hour to 72 miles per hour.

1962: Fuel gauge added to instruments.

1966: 1,300-cc engine installed, generator replaced by alternator, air cleaner moved, light and wiper switches moved to left side of speedometer.

1967: 1,500-cc engine installed, 53 horsepower available, front disc brakes make optional, and top speed increased to 82 miles per hour.

1968: Semi-automatic transmission with hydraulic torque converter made optional.

1969: Double-jointed halfshaft rear suspension made available with semi-automatic.

1970: 1,600-cc engine made optional.

1972: 2.5-miles-per-hour bumpers and padded steering wheel used.

1973: Discs made standard on 1600, 6x15-inch tires used.

Sergio Satorelli's 1500 Karmann-Ghia, 1962. Based on the Type 3, it was not a success. This model is rare today in any part of the world.

The convertible was introduced in 1957, and was just as well-balanced visually as the coupe. The convertible also had the benefit of Karmann's luxurious tops, which were well padded, smooth, and weatherproof. In 1964–1965, like the Beetle Convertible, the Ghia convertible got a new vinyl top, which folded more compactly. And like its sibling, it was also an immediate success. Again, expect to pay more for a convertible than a coupe in like condition.

The rarest of all production Karmann-Ghias was the Type 3 1500. Designed by Ghia's Sergio Satorelli, It was a strange combination of Corvair, Dodge Dart,

and VW. Not altogether unpleasant, but not a market success either, it saw only 42,432 units produced from 1962 to 1969. A more pleasing convertible version was built but never saw production. Poor attention to detail was noticed by *Road & Track* testers, and few nice words could be mustered regarding the new design. The car was neither much faster, at 87 miles per hour, nor better than its smaller sibling; cost more; and was never as pretty. The question was, why bother? Few people did. For some, however, it would make an unusual addition to a collection of VWs. A mint one, at the right price, might be desirable.

Chapter 8

Special-Bodied Type 1 Cars 1949–1968

★★★★★
Hebmüller
★★★★★
Rometsch
★★★★★
Denzel
★★★★★
Dannenhauser
★★★★★
Strauss, Eller, Drews
★★★★
Enzmann
★★★
MCA Jetstar
★★★
Devin

The history of the special-bodied Type 1 VWs is a large subject and worthy of an entire book alone. Here, however, is a brief review, limited to the special VWs bodied by coachbuilders or manufacturers, leaving out the dune buggies and replicars. Also missing in this account are the many one-offs still to be discovered. A two-door coupe, à la Hebmüller, was restored in England by Beetle buff Bob Shaill. The Shaill VW has a special body by Stoll.

Right up front, potential buyers must be aware that any of the special-bodied cars will present far more restoration problems than any production VW. Body and interior parts are, in most cases, not available and will have to be fabricated. Some lights, trim items, knobs, seats, and so forth may be the same as those used on other German cars of the era–BMW, DKW, Borgward–but will nevertheless be difficult to find. At this time, it is usually far less expensive to buy a properly restored special-bodied VW than to pay virtually nothing for a rusty basket case and send it to a restoration shop. These are cars for the serious, financially flush collector only.

Hebmüller

Remember two things about the Hebmüllers: Perhaps as many as 12 of the later convertibles were produced by Karmann, and Hebmüller also made a coupe, but reportedly the only example was destroyed in an accident.

A Hebmüller with its hood up. The higher roofline smoothed out the shape, making the car better-looking with the top up than down.

Before the Hebmüller era, Colonel C. R. Radclyffe, a British commander, ordered this two-seat convertible from the war-torn VW plant.

The Radclyffe design, as interpreted by Hebmüller. Production began in 1949, then stopped in 1952, after only 696 were built.

From 1949 to the summer of 1952, the small Hebmüller firm turned out approximately 696 two-seater Beetle Convertibles of exceedingly nice proportions. That they are convertibles, rare, and exceptionally attractive means they are also very much in demand and highly prized.

Rometsch

Equally collectible are cars in the series of Rometsch convertibles built from the early 1950s to around 1960. At least four variations of these luxuriously rebodied VWs were produced. The first Rometschs garnered the nickname "The Banana" owing to their rounded, elongated shape. A coupe

and a convertible were offered, both with a single, sideways rear seat. Reportedly, around 500 were constructed before 1956.

In 1956, Rometsch restyled its design along the lines of an American car, with a wraparound windshield and an outlandish two-tone treatment. The vehicle would have been in direct competition with VW's new Karmann-Ghia, and the supply of chassis for the Rometsch ceased. Rometsch, however, continued to produce a limited number of cars until 1961.

The Berlin coachbuilder also produced around 50 four-door Beetles, some of which were used as taxis in Berlin. Any Rometsch is a highly desirable collectible, and, apparently, a fair number of the later cars were imported to the United States.

Denzel

The Denzel was the car that could have been a Porsche. Wolfgang Denzel, a wealthy sportsman from Vienna, Austria, constructed about 160 cars from 1949 to 1961. Denzels used highly modified VW engines in the 1300 and 1500 versions, and later turned to 1,600-cc Porsche units for the last few cars. The frames and bodies were hand-built and used typical Italian *superleggera* techniques to attach the steel and aluminum body to the framework. Denzels were successful rally cars, and in the United States they made a great impression in Sports Car Club of America racing, being generally faster than the Porsches. Denzel cranks, pistons, liners, and cams were also sold as VW modification kits. Six or seven Denzels were in the United States at last count.

Dannenhauser

Dannenhauser was a small firm that attempted to create production custom Beetles in the early 1950s. Few examples were built, fewer survived, and fewer yet were ever imported to the United States.

Stauss, Eller, Drews

Like Dannenhauser, Stauss, Eller, Drews attempted to produce custom Beetles in the early 1950s; only a few were ever finished.

The one-off Hebmüller coupe. Its whereabouts are unknown. The prototype, even from the rear, looks interesting and attractive.

Enzmann

Fiberglass cars are in a class by themselves. Most are home-built from kits, and quality varies tremendously. Buying a special-bodied VW such as a Rometsch is much different than purchasing a Fiberfab. The better-known fiberglass cars include examples from Enzmann, MCA Jetstar, and Devin.

A Swiss doctor wanted something different, and came up with the Enzmann, a strange-looking, doorless creation. Footwells were provided in the side of the fiberglass-reinforced resin body to aid entrance. The hardtop–presumably down while someone enters the car–was raised from the rear of the vehicle. Reportedly, around 100 such cars were made and sold between 1957 and 1968. On the plus side, Enzmanns were fast, most using OKRASA tuning kits or MAG superchargers.

MCA Jetstar

Either the MCA Jetstar, built in the early 1960s in Breman, Germany, was equipped with a Devin-supplied body, or MCA took a mold from a Devin for this two-seater. Variations of VW powerplants were offered, and perhaps 100 cars were built.

Devin

Devin perhaps built a few quasi-production cars based on the VW. But Bill Devin also did not design the famous, familiar, and versatile fiberglass body. He took a mold from a rare Italian Ermini around 1954. Those who live in fiberglass houses . . .

Devin's next creation of note was the famous dune buggy: He was not only imaginative, but well ahead of his time. His success inspired many firms, such as Fiberfab, which was still going strong in the early 1990s.

The boom era of the fiberglass body, from the mid-1950s to 1970, coincided with the boom in sports cars, the do-it-yourself craze, and a wealth of good, used, inexpensive VW chassis. At the same time, the traditional coachbuilders–Hebmüller, Rometsch, and firms such as Denzel–found it increasingly difficult to continue to hand-build cars. But perhaps the most significant reason fiberglass bodies were popular then was the success of VW's own special-bodied car, the Karmann-Ghia, introduced in 1955. New VW chassis were no longer delivered to eager coachbuilders, and in the place of coachbuilder specials came the fiberglass home-built specials.

Replicars

VW-based replicars range from the fiberglass "Bugatti" to the "Alfa Romeo," the "Frazer-Nash,"

Is the Denzel a VW? Not according to Wolfgang Denzel, who used the concept and the engine to produce Porsche eaters. Aluminum bodies and special hand-built frames made a big difference.

and coupes such as the Bradley GT. These can be a great deal of fun for the money. However, they are often poorly constructed, difficult to get past safety inspections, and for summer use only. They cannot be entered in vintage events or serious shows, and they will rarely be appreciated. Buy one with these caveats in mind, and perhaps you will not be disappointed.

Chapter 9

★★★★
1950–1967
Transporter, Pickup, Kombi, Microbus

★★
1968–1978
Panel Truck, Pickup, Kombi, Campmobile, Station Wagon

★★
1979–1991 Kombi, Vanagon, Van, Pickup

★★★
1991–1999 EuroVan, Weekender, Winnebago

Transporter, Kombi, Microbus, Vanagon, and EuroVan 1950–1999

Ben Pon was a Dutchman who, despite harboring some rather hard feelings about the German invasion of the Netherlands in World War II, believed in the concept of the VW. Nor was he averse to getting rich–which he did. Pon successfully sold the early VWs in his native country, and in 1949, was chosen to bring the first VW to the United States–which he did with less success.

Two years earlier, Pon had sketched the plans for the VW Type 2, a Transporter-van based on the Beetle chassis and drivetrain. However, it was not until 1950 that production actually started. The proliferation of models began almost immediately. From one basic box came the Kombi, camper, pickup, Microbus, Transporter, ambulance, fire truck, station wagon, Vanagon, Wasserboxer, and a host of other variations and names. Yet despite the variety of models, the Transporter had only three major model changes from 1950 to 1990. The VW van was the last VW with a rear engine—60 a flat-four, albeit water-cooled. Pon's basic concept was at last dispensed with in 1991, when VW launched the front-drive EuroVan.

1950–1967

Although almost two million VW vans were built between 1950 and 1967, as with the sedan, these earlier models rank highest among

Before the EuroVan came three generations of VW Transporters, called the Type 2: the 1950–1966 model, upper left; the 1967–1978 version, upper right; and the 1979–1990 Vanagon, foreground.

The camper could be had with almost every conceivable option, including a portable john. Note the wheel stand for the table. VW Transporters did not catch on in the United States until the 1960s.

collectors. Charm, rarity, and their embodiment of an era make them more desirable. However, the later the van, the better the vehicle, in terms of power, handling, and comfort.

As with the Beetle, few examples made it to the United States before 1954. Sales were as slow as the car itself. In 1956, only three models were offered: the basic Kombi, Microbus, and Microbus Deluxe. By the 1960s, however, the American public had become enamored–the popular Microbus was, after all, the first "minivan." More models were imported to meet the demand, and prices were actually reduced. In 1963, the following models were available:
• Panel delivery truck (Transporter), $1,895
• Pickup truck, $1,885
• Pickup truck with double cab (six-seater), $2,175
• Kombi station wagon with seats, $2,095
• Kombi station wagon with sunroof, $2,220
• Station wagon (often known as the Microbus), $2, 399
• Deluxe station wagon, $2,655

In addition to the standard models, six camper options were offered to outfit the Kombi and the panel truck with special windows, interior panels made of birch, double beds, closets, curtains, shelves, refrigerators, water storage tanks, chemical toilets, and gas stoves. Further individual options included tents, showers, sun decks, and luggage racks, to name a few. The Westfalia company was the outfitter of choice for Deluxe camper versions. Westfalia was founded in 1844 and continued to provide VW camping versions with the 1992 Weekender–certainly maintaining a long and fruitful relationship.

All versions of the VW bus used virtually the same overall dimensions, although the Microbus Deluxe was 1 inch longer than others. The wheelbase on all models was 94.5 inches; the length was 168.5 inches for all but the Microbus Deluxe, for which it was 169.5 inches;

"Getting Away from It All" was the camper theme back in the 1960s, and this artist's depiction featured automotive camping through the twentieth century. It remains a valid theme for the new EuroVan.

With its popularity soaring and a well-established market, VW introduced the second series in 1967 for the 1968 model year. They remained outwardly identical, aside from minor lighting changes. This is a 1968–1969 Transporter.

and although the height depended on the options, standard was 75.8 inches. Weights varied from 2,359 pounds for the panel truck to 2,535 pounds for the Deluxe station wagon, and up for campers. The total permissible weight was pegged at 4,564 pounds. Payload, then, averaged around 2,000 pounds.

Since 1950, the series had come equipped with the 1200 engine, giving from 25 to 40 horsepower and making it woefully inadequate for U.S. driving conditions, particularly when fully loaded. *Road & Track's* 1956 Microbus fully loaded took 75 seconds to hit 60 miles per hour, which was also its top speed. This poor acceleration should be a prime consideration when purchasing an older VW van, bus, or camper today. The vehicle offered no savings in gas mileage, either. Few buses ever topped 30 miles per gallon, but that was not bad for the era, or the size and usefulness of the vehicle.

The aging 1200 (1,192 cc) was replaced in 1963–1964 with the 1500 (1,493 cc) from the Type 11 series. It helped, but not a great deal. The 0–60-miles-per-hour time was reduced, but the quarter-mile still took 25 seconds. The top speed was nearly 70 miles per hour. The lack of power led to a multitude of engine swaps–another concern for the would-be buyer. Remember, too, that all transmissions were the standard four-speed VW issue, but with stump-pulling ratios. Also for your information: Most pre-1967 vans came equipped with gear-reduction hubs on each rear axle.

The best bets with the VW Transporters are fully optioned 1963–1967 campers; rare six-passenger double-cab pickups; the high-topped delivery van, which was not generally available in the United States; and any special industrial conversion. More popular were the Microbus Deluxes, with two-tone paint, chrome bumpers, skylights, and a fabric sunroof. Rarity, options, and originality are key watchwords with early buses.

1968–1978

The theme was the same for 1968–1978, but the 1968 VW Transporter, still known as the Type 2, was an all-new vehicle. Of the different dimensions, only the wheelbase remained the same. The new box was 5.5 inches longer, almost 1 inch wider, and averaged 1 inch taller than the one on the earlier model. The new Transporters were also 100 pounds heavier. The tire size was now 5x14 inches. Major visual differences were reflected in the glass. The one-piece wraparound windshield was 27 percent larger, and the longer, larger side windows were vented. The old double doors were replaced by a sliding door, a full 41.7 inches wide. Up front was what appeared to be a grille, but the long series of vents below the windshield were air intakes for an improved ventilation system. Sunroofs were now all metal.

This vehicle still had little competition. The small vans from Chevy and Ford never caught on, Japan was light years away, and the Chrysler Mini-Vans were not even a twinkle in Lee Iacocca's eye. The list of safety features designed into the new van was a clear signal that VW was intent on staying in the increasingly lucrative U.S. market. A deep-dished steering wheel; a padded dashboard with recessed dials and nonreflective interior surfaces; padded visor, armrests, seat tops, and handbrake; an impact-absorbing outside mirror; rubber-covered control knobs; an improved wiper system; and a full double-jointed rear suspension were all now standard. Even the new engine could–or should–have been considered a safety feature.

Still using the flat-four Type 3 engine, displacement increased to 1,600 cc (1,584 cc), and power to 57 horsepower. Gas mileage ratings and the top speed remained the same, but the increased torque of the 1600 was sorely needed. The 0–60-miles-per-hour time was down to a mere 37 seconds, which was a big improvement on the 1956 time of 75 seconds but still on a par with the ill-fated Subaru 360's acceleration.

VW now decided to separate the trucks from the station wagons. Perhaps it was easier to keep track of the multitude of models, options, and styles by doing so. For 1968, the models and prices were as follows:

Station Wagons
- Seven-seater, $2,495
- Nine-seater, $2,517
- Kombi with center and rear seats, $2,265
- Basic Campmobile, $2,110

Trucks
- Panel truck, single side door, $2,295
- Panel truck, double side door, $2,395

The new bus had a large, 41-inch-wide side opening, which replaced the old double-door setup of the first series.

A 1979 camper, ready to hit the wilderness. This had the Westfalia raising top, which added much space to the interior. Late-1970s colors left something to be desired.

The third-series Type 2, introduced in 1979, was perhaps the most attractive of the rear-engine Transporters. And again, it continued through the production run with few outward changes. This 1987 Wolfsburg Limited Edition has special wheels and interior.

The interior of the 1987 Vanagon GL Wolfsburg Limited Edition was both modern and sumptuous. Prices started at $10,000 in 1980 and continued to climb through the 1980s.

The dashboard of the Vanagon was much more carlike than that of earlier vans, and it was comfortable and offered good visibility. This is the 1986 camper.

• Pickup truck, single cab, $2,295
• Pickup truck, double cab, $2,385

Options included white-sidewall tires ($29.50); a driver's vent window ($15); a third vent in passenger's compartment ($11); and a range of camping options ($655 to $1,075), with the most expensive providing a pop-up roof and tent. The box was new, but the contents were more of the same.

The 1971 models were bestowed with 3 more horsepower; they were still carbureted, but featured a dual-port manifold, and for the first time front servo-assisted disc brakes, a great improvement over the old drums, were offered.

The 1972 models had the 1700 (1,679 cc) 411 engine installed, and suddenly the performance was acceptable. The powerplant's 74 horsepower meant 0–60 miles per hour in 22 seconds and the quarter-mile in 23 seconds, with a top speed of 75 miles per hour.

A three-speed automatic transmission was first made available in the 1973. It cost $235 more but, remarkable, did not affect straight-line performance.

Well-matched, well-geared, and well-engineered, the automatic performed to nearly identical specs compared with the standard four-speed.

In 1973, VW began to rate horsepower in net versus gross figures, resulting in dismay and confusion. This meant the 74-horsepower 1700 was now rated at 65 horsepower. The 1800 engine of 1974 was rated at 67 horsepower, thanks to a new electronic fuel injection system, and in 1975, the van was equipped with the same full 2-liter engine as the Porsche 914. Horsepower remained the same but was produced at a lower rpm, enabling the van to cover the quarter-mile in 21.6 seconds and do 0–60 miles per hour in 19.9 seconds. As performance increased, so did prices. Even the lowly Kombi was listed at $5,195 in 1975, a portent of things to come.

What the second series, the van and the Kombi, gained in speed and practicality, it lost in charm. Don't look for these to be collectible–at least not within the average lifetime–but they can provide low-cost, economical, and enjoyable transportation.

The 1986 camper interior reflected good taste and convenience, with speakers, curtains, and sliding windows. The Vanagon had only two problems: a falling dollar and the still-underpowered rear engine.

The 1989 Vanagons featured more side protection with restyled lower moldings. This is the short-lived Carat version.

The interior of 1989 Wolfsburg Editions was often decked out in a wild pattern. Still, it looks comfortable despite the stripes.

1979–1991

Entering the 1980s, VW made a surprising announcement: The new VW station wagon-van-Kombi would retain the rear-drive flat-four configuration. It was claimed that the old layout freed 68 percent of the space the vehicle occupied on the road for cargo, versus 56 percent in most other conventional vans; that the rear-engined layout was superior in hill climbing with marginal traction; and that access to the rear compartment from the front was easy. History will judge that decision; suffice it to say that by the mid-1980s, Lee Iacocca's MiniVans were eating the VWs for lunch and had captured the market that VW had established and maintained for so many years.

Nonetheless, the third-series vans were no doubt the best ever, and with the availability of the Syncro, even downright exciting. As with the second series, the new van was all-new, but this time, the dimensions were identical save the width, which was 3.3 inches greater. The windshield was deeper and had more rake, the side windows were larger, and the rear window had doubled in size. This design also featured a grille—not a ventilation intake, but a grille—up front, which hinted at the water-cooled diesel and gas engines to come. Inside, the layout was much more car-like, and again, all-new.

Six standard versions were available: two vans, two Kombis, and two pickups. In the United States, only two models were imported: the seven- and nine-seat Vanagon and a stripped-down Kombi, to be used as a base for the Westfalia camping options. Initially, the existing 2-liter 67-horsepower fuel-injected engine was the only choice in the United States, using either the three-speed automatic or four-speed standard gearbox.

What should have happened in 1980 occurred in 1991: The new EuroVan was finally front engined, front drive. Equipped with the 2,459-cc single-overhead-cam five-cylinder engine, it was rated at 109 horsepower.

The EuroVan continued the Type 2 tradition with panel Transporters, vans (here called Caravelles), pickup trucks, and campers. VW, however, was calling the new van the T4, for the fourth Transporter type.

Gone was the old Porsche front suspension, replaced by unequal-length A-arms and variable-rate coil springs. The double-jointed rear end was retained but augmented by variable-rate coil springs, and the combination created the safest VW van yet, with the best handling to date. The vehicle's weight was up to 3,290 pounds, and the price was up too, to just under $10,000 for the Vanagon L model. The gas mileage was down, however, and most 2-liter vans were only good for 16 to 23 miles per gallon.

Road & Track found the new Vanagon much to its liking and claimed that it proved, once again, VW's position as the "manufacturer of the world's leading van." The writers did caution readers to be very careful of the oil filter tube located behind the rear license plate. It seems that pump jocks often missed the location of the fuel filler flap near the right front door and proceeded to lift the rear plate and fill the oil tube with gas.

The promised diesel appeared for European van enthusiasts in 1982, with the 1,588-cc passenger-car unit rated at around 50 horsepower for the van. It was as good on fuel consumption as it was bad on

The MV option included full wheel covers, two rear-facing removable jump seats, and point velour seat covering. The rear seats could also be folded forward to become a bed, or could be removed altogether.

The lines are attractive, but photos make the EuroVan appear much smaller than it is. The EuroVan was, by design, a large, midsize van rather that a minivan. The GL option included a premium cassette stereo and dual air conditioning.

performance. It could get better than 30 miles per gallon, but like the Transporters of old was lacking in acceleration and top speed.

The need for a more efficient, quieter powerplant encouraged the development of a water-cooled flat-four "Wasserboxer," which was introduced in 1983–1984. The 1,915-cc engine was virtually new, now having an additional 15 horsepower and getting nearly 20 percent better fuel economy.

A larger, 2,110-cc version with 95 horsepower powered the Syncro in 1986, a van that now did

The EuroVan was the only van to offer four-wheel independent suspension, and it also came with a unique Load-sensitive Braking System (LBS) that adjusted the brakes for cargo weight, to help prevent rear wheel lockup.

everything and everywhere. Perhaps the Syncro will be the last significant development in a design concept that has seen steady production for over 40 years. For buyers thinking in terms of today's use and tomorrow's worth, the Vanagon Syncro camper might just be the best ticket in town.

1991–1993 EuroVan

Having exhausted the potentials of the Vanagon, Volkswagen introduced the EuroVan series at the Boston Auto Show in late 1991. It began appearing in small numbers in dealer showrooms in late 1992 for the 1993 model year. VW called this the T4, indicating the fourth generation of Volkswagen vans.

The EuroVan was a complete break with the past. Gone was the rear-engined four. The new model brought the Transporter group into line with a transverse front-wheel drive chassis, and VW went to great lengths to maximize the interior space while keeping the overall dimensions "midsized." As VW stated, the EuroVan was to compete with truck-based passenger vans, such as the Chevrolet Astro and Ford Aerostar. This too was a break with the past. The dimensions were imposing, with an overall height of 74.8 inches. While driving the EuroVan, it was possible to literally look down at conventional minivans, yet it was only two inches longer than a Honda Accord. Gone was the boxy shape associated with the older vans, but the driving position was still very bus-like. *Road & Track* tested the EuroVan in 1994, and found that " . . . the steering column is canted sharply upward, for that authentic VW Microbus driving position." Fifteen-inch wheels were equipped with 205/65R tires. Brakes were ventilated discs up front and drums in the rear; an antilock braking system was an option. Steering was power-assisted rack and pinion.

The only engine offered was the 2,459-cc SOHC five, with Digifant fuel injection and three-way catalytic converter, mated to either a five-speed manual or optional four-speed automatic. The output was only 109 horsepower, and despite the 140 pounds of torque available, the EuroVan was underpowered. It took almost 20 seconds to reach 60 miles per hour, and top speed with a tail wind was around 90 miles per hour. With almost 4,400 pounds to propel, the VR6 would have been a better choice, at least for American markets. The five didn't offer any substantial gas savings either. The EuroVan was EPAed at 15/19, city/highway, and actual mileage figures were very similar.

But the EuroVan was aiming at a more specific market. The most significant feature was the space utilization, which offered an unusual amount of inside capacity. Making this possible was a new unitized frame, with double wishbone front suspension, rather than the tall MacPherson struts. Torsion bars also saved space. At the rear, semitrailing arms with coil springs provided independent suspension without encroaching on internal space dimensions. This concentration on space management enabled the EuroVan to boast an interior volume of 201 cubic feet of space, as measured from behind the front seat with all other seats removed. Compared with the competition, the EuroVan provided more space than all but the longest Fords and Chevys, and 35 percent more than the average minivan.

Three trim packages were offered, the CL, GL, and MV. Standard equipment on all three models included full carpeting, beverage holders, full cloth seats, front and rear air conditioning, front and rear heating, tinted glass, and power mirrors. The traditional Westfalia camper, now called the Weekender, took advantage of the ample interior room. Available with the MV option, the Weekender package included a "pop top" roof, a two-person bed, window screens, electric refrigerator, a second battery, and window curtains. The installation of the rear air conditioning was not possible with the Weekender, and the heat generated from the exhaust system meant that the rear passenger section could get rather warm in summer. *Road & Track* also noted that the EuroVan was noisy, at least by car standards. Overall, they found it comfortable and a ". . . bridge between the worlds of obligation and leisure . . . . You may not actually pack a stove and split, but you could if you wanted to. And it's that capability that makes it attractive." In 1994, the list price was $21,850, and $27,385 with the Weekender package.

In 1995, the Weekender concept was placed directly in the hands of Winnebago Industries, one of the oldest manufacturers of RV trailers and motorhomes. Extended wheelbase EuroVans were shipped to Forest City, Iowa, where Winnebago outfitted them with a screened pop-up top, overhead bunks, benches, closets, and everything including a kitchen sink. A two-burner gas stove and an LP gas refrigerator were neatly designed into the package, and the addition of utility tables, AC to DC power converter, and a 12-gallon fresh-water tank made the EuroVan ready to go anywhere, for any period of time.

Advertising was literally word of mouth. The EuroVan Camper Winnebago was, as of 1998, still available through selected dealers.

The Winnebago variant began with an extended-wheelbase van. Winnebago then added the top, sink, fridge, and stove to come up with a complete camper. This apparently was the only version of the EuroVan offered in the U.S. after 1995, and could be ordered through Winnebago of Forest City, Iowa.

Vanagon and EuroVan Comparison

	Vanagon	EuroVan
Wheelbase	97 in	115 in
Length	179.9 in	186.6 in
Width	72.6 in	72.4 in
Height	75.9 in	75.2 in
Weight	3,290 lb	3,800 lb (estimated)
Rear-door load height	32 in	20 in
Power	90 hp	109 hp
Torque	117 lb-ft at 3,300 rpm	144 lb-ft at 2,200 rpm
Fuel tank capacity	15.5 gal	121 gal
Gas mileage	19 mpg highway	21 mpg highway
Drag coefficient	0.45	0.36

Chapter 10

★★★★
1941–1945
Kübelwagen
★★★★
1942–1944
Schwimmwagen
★★★
1960–1979
The Thing

World War II interrupted Porsche's plans for a people's car, as production was shifted in 1939 to military vehicles. The KdF Type 87 had four-wheel drive, tractor-like tires, and a roller in front to protect it from large bumps.

Kübelwagen, Schwimmwagen and The Thing 1941–1975

Kübelwagen and The Thing are interesting names for a couple of VW's most interesting vehicles. The Kübelwagen of the World War II years was mimicked 30-odd years later by the 1969–1975 Thing. One might view The Thing as a factory replicar, updated to meet modern but minimal requirements.

Kübelwagen and Schwimmwagen

Wartime Kübelwagens were Germany's Jeep equivalent. Hitler's new factory was finished just in time to convert production of the new people's car to that of military vehicles. The VW chassis, it was thought, would make an ideal basis for a general-purpose military vehicle. Accordingly, the Porsche design staff created the Type 82, an open box structure with straight, rigid body panels, very tub-like in appearance. The name Kübelwagen, or Tub Car, quickly took root.

Few mechanical differences separated the civilian VW and Kübelwagen. The primary changes on the Kübelwagen were a larger, 25-horse-

As the Allies managed to cut short the supply of petroleum to Germany, military vehicles were modified to operate on wood and charcoal. This is the typical Type 82, or Kübelwagen.

power 1,130-cc engine; reduction drive gears placed behind each rear wheel; a limited-slip differential; a small, lightweight transmission; and later, four-wheel drive. When reviewing the following list of VW-based wartime vehicles, keep in mind that actual production numbers are hard to confirm.

The Type 82 standard Kübelwagen came with two-wheel drive, limited-slip, and reduction gears. Some were equipped with normal VW drive components. A total 48,000 were produced from 1941–1945.

The Type 166 Schwimmwagen Amphibious designed for use on the Russian front had four-wheel drive with a propeller. A total 15,500 were produced between 1942 and 1944.

The Type 128 Kübelwagen four-wheel-drive version saw 750 produced in 1944–1945.

The Type 87 Beetle sedan with four-wheel drive saw 750 produced in 1944–1945.

The Type 82E Beetle sedan with two-wheel drive, limited-slip, and hub reduction gears saw 1,500 built from 1943–1945.

Records also indicate that approximately 2,000 of the 986-cc KdF Beetles were made from 1940–1943 for military use, and 1,000 of the 1,130-cc versions from 1943–1945.

Generally, the Kübelwagens that were captured and analyzed by the Allies got impressive reviews. It was not quite a match for the all-American jeep, but Germany's prime military service vehicle was based on a civilian chassis with few changes. Although propriety and propaganda demanded moderation in their assessment, Allied engineers found favor with the widespread use of aluminum, the unique limited-slip, the all-independent suspension, and the special transmission, plus the design's ability to stand up well in all conditions from the African desert to the Russian winter.

The American foot soldier got a slightly different story. From *The German Soldier*, a military training manual of 1943:

"Here, side by side, you see the two most popular vehicles of the war—one, an American jeep; the other, a German VW . . .

"Captured VWs have been tested and they are nothing to brag about. They have two-wheel drive and the jeep is four-wheel.

"The suspension and general construction don't permit the tough cross-country driving the jeep can

Huge lumps also appeared on the Type 82E, which was not equipped with four-wheel drive.

The Schwimmwagen in action. Designated the Type 166, this vehicle could go literally anywhere. Most examples, however, went to the Russian front. These were a remarkable adaptation of the humble Beetle.

take. We make them better and faster . . . . The main reason for the success of German motorized equipment in campaigns ranging from the plain of Poland to the mountains of Greece is preventive maintenance by the German soldier."

After the war, Kübelwagens served as basic transportation for many German civilians, but were discarded as quickly as possible because they were reminders of a war that went badly for the German people. Military vehicle collectors purchased the remainders.

Although Kübelwagens are not very streetable, they can be shown at military meets as well as car shows like the annual Bug Outs. Konrad F. Schreier, a Kübelwagen collector, rents his fleet out to film companies for movies like *The Battle of Britain*. At

The four-wheel drive on captured Type 166 KdFs, totally versatile and easy to repair, impressed the Allies far more than they wrote. Reportedly, 15,500 Type 166 KdFs were produced from 1942–1944.

any rate, despite the high cost (the last Kübelwagen I saw advertised was $25,000), Germany's jeep can be an enjoyable collectible.

The Thing

The Thing could have been some-Thing else. In 1969, with a focus on German armed forces, an updated Kübelwagen, designated the Type 181, was introduced. The concept and style were virtually identical to those of the original Kübelwagen, and the main visual differences were squared-off fenders and wheel openings versus the Kübelwagen's rounded, almost cycle fenders. Unfortunately, the Type 181 did not feature four-wheel drive, or even a limited-slip. Initially, it did have the reduction gear hub of the Kübelwagens, but that was phased out. The German military bought a few examples, but the Type 181 could not compete with more modern, four-wheel-drive competitors.

VW refocused, this time with the United States in mind. With new, bright colors (but finished in semigloss paint), 14x5-inch wheels, and a new name, The Thing was launched. It made use of the Transporter suspension, gearbox, and 46-horsepower 1 600-cc dual-port head, and did the quarter-mile in 22 seconds. A gas heater from the 412 was standard equipment. The Thing, like the Kübelwagen, was a four-door bucket with a large folding top and side curtains–the latter being something even the British had given up on by 1962. Interestingly, though The Thing was totally developed in Germany, all production was out of Mexico.

Like the Kübelwagen of the past, it should have been sold with four-wheel drive. This would have made it more serviceable to a larger group of buyers interested in the outdoors. The most serious problem was the price. *Road & Track's* price as tested

The Type 166 propeller has a collapsible linkage and was engaged to the engine crankshaft by a dog clutch. Examples of these are desirable military collectibles, but they are very difficult to find.

The reincarnation of the Kübelwagen was The Thing, designed for the German armed forces. Designated the Type 181, it did not fare well in the military, but Mexican-made The Things sold in the United States between 1972–1979

in 1973 was a whopping $2,858. No matter that The Thing was more expensive than the Super Beetle; what puts the price in perspective is that in 1973, a new BMW 2002 could be had for as little as $3,600, and The Thing was perceived as almost minimal transportation, rather than a useful, all-around vehicle. It is possible that equipped with four-wheel drive and even brighter colors, The Thing would have given the AMC-Chrysler Jeep some competition during the boom years of

1985–1990, but by 1979, VW's The Thing was a thing of the past.

Today, I always take a second look when a Thing goes by–which rarely occurs. Most are tatty, beat, driven by teenagers, and begging to be restored. These machines rust like tubs, their tops and interiors are bygones, and mechanically, they need everything. But they also can be bought with few dollars. The Thing is a best bet for a future collectible.

Chapter 11

Type 3 1961–1973

By 1955, it was obvious even to Heinz Nordhoff that the Beetle, no matter how successful, would need a replacement. While wanting a more upmarket product, Nordhoff also wished to retain the features that made the Beetle famous. More room was needed, and for that reason, the new car would have to be based on the traditional three-box shape. Another Nordhoff requirement was that the new chassis would have the same wheelbase as the Beetle. A station wagon model was also planned, and that in turn required a flatter engine than the normal 1200, with its high cooling fan.

By 1957, the Type 3 was on the drawing boards and the engineers would eventually achieve everything Nordhoff asked for. Still, the project was postponed several times because, according to Jan P. Norbye (*VW Treasures by Karmann*), "every time Nordhoff weighed the question of when to start tooling up for the new car, he looked at the Beetle sales statistics, whose strength was most reassuring, and the urgency of getting the proposed Beetle replacement into production never became evident to him." The Beetle was a hard act to follow. Not until 1961 was the Type 3 ready for the dealers, and Nordhoff's procrastination would prove to be the first in a series of near-fatal errors.

The 1600 Type 3 arrived in the United States only as a station wagon and a fastback in late 1965. It was recognizable as a VW product despite the square shape.

73

Heinz Nordhoff's upmarket VW took shape as the 1,500-cc Type 3. Perhaps most impressive was the roomier and more luxurious interior of the 1500 notchback, or sedan, with large comfortable seats, a full instrument panel, and full carpets.

The Type 3 was the first truly new car to roll out of Wolfsburg. The chassis used the traditional transverse torsion bar, with dual trailing links up front and swing axles in the rear. There were no surprises here. The engine, however, boasted a new cooling fan arrangement, driven directly off the crankshaft, and lowering the electrical accessories allowed the station wagon version–known in Germany as the Variant–to have a sufficiently low floor. The platform backbone chassis was very similar to that of the old Beetle.

When the Type 3 was finally in production, Nordhoff decided that it would not replace the Beetle after all. The car's reception was warm but not overwhelming. It was, perhaps, too little, too late. The Type 3 was not imported to the United States until 1965–1966. By then, the displacement had increased to 1,584 cc, and power was up to 65 horsepower. A further improvement was the addition of front disc brakes, although none had servo-assist.

Left
The 1966 Type 3s offered disc brakes in the front, which the old Beetle never had, at least Stateside.

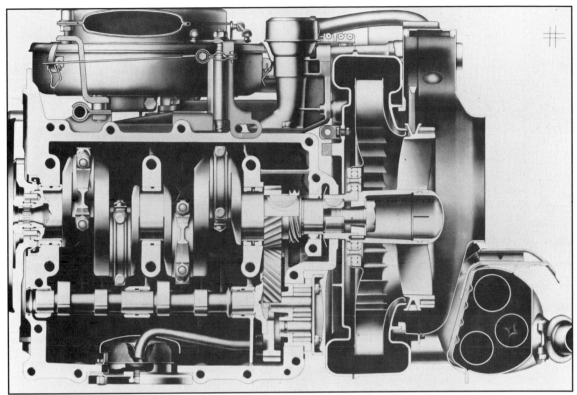

A good cutaway of the new flat-four developed for the Type 3. The cooling fan was driven off the front of the crankshaft and allowed a much lower profile.

The 1966 fastback was the least attractive of the three models offered, the rear appearing as a poor attempt to streamline the car. Although the fastback was larger than the Beetle, the wheelbase remained the same at 94.5 inches.

Beetle and Type 3 Comparison

	1300 VW Sedan	1500 Type 3 Sedan
Wheelbase	94.5 in	94.5 in
Length	166.8 in	166.3 in
Width	60.8 in	63.2 in
Height	59 in	58.1 in
Weight	1,760 lb	1,940 lb
Horsepower	50 hp	54 hp
Torque	70 lb-ft at 2,000 rpm	83 lb-ft at 2,800 rpm
Displacement	1,285 cc	1,493 cc
Bore x stroke	3.03x2.72 in	3.27x2.72 in
Brakes	four-wheel drum	four-wheel drum
Top speed	75 mph	81 mph

The Type 3 was offered in three forms: a two-door sedan; the Variant, which was called the squareback in the United States; and the TL, called the fastback in the United States. Only the squareback and fastback were imported to the States, but plenty of gray-market sedans made their way in via Canada and Germany, and many can be found today.

As expected, the Type 3 was more expensive than the Beetle. At a time when a 1300 sedan could be had for under $2,000 new, the fastback was listed at $2,454, and the squareback at around $2,550. A sunroof–all metal now–was one of the few options.

VW anticipated that 1 in 10 of all VWs sold in the States would buy Type 3s.

In 1968, the 1600 was available with an automatic transmission; a revised double-jointed rear suspension, with the automatic only; and fuel injection. The revised suspension was, according to *Road & Track*, a mixed blessing. The old torsion bar front suspension, designed specifically for a swing-axle rear suspension, was retained, causing initial understeer, making low-speed turning difficult for the front tires. But the Bosch fuel injection received high praise from all quarters, being touted by *Road and Track* as "the model of what a

The 1967 Type 3s featured a dual braking system, different gear ratios, dual back-up lights, and retractable lap belts. The 1969s got a slight facelift before VW buried them.

The unique position of the fastback dipstick made it all too easy for pump jockeys to think it was the gas filler. Access to the engine was, to say the least, limited.

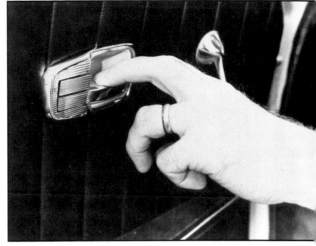

Nice touches on the inside door handles of the Type 3. The lower section included the pull handle, and the lock was positioned above and to the rear.

fuel injection system ought to be." The price was up, of course, to $2,770 for the squareback.

In Europe, the Type 3 had teething troubles–as many new cars did then. And in the United States, buyers found out all too quickly that the new VWs rusted even faster than the Beetles, and that the fenders and running boards could no longer be simply unbolted and replaced. Although more comprehensive, the interiors were of the same quality as the Beetle's, and vinyl was soon sagging and splitting. Access to the engine was difficult, and the new fuel injection was more costly to repair than carburetion.

The 1969 models got a slight face-lift, but few other changes were in the offing. Nordhoff died in 1968, and the Type 3 was just marking time. Production of the Type 3 ceased in 1973, after 2,583,015 had rolled off the line.

It is difficult to judge the overall value of the Type 3. Not popular when new, these cars did not have the charm or reputation of the Beetle. They are still decreasing in numbers, as they are not yet old enough or sought after enough to be saved to obtain, particularly body panels, although engines are readily bought. Yet, historically, the Type 3 is important. A Type 3 could be a sound, enjoyable investment if it is near mint at a reasonable price.

The most collectible Type 3 would have to be the Karmann convertible constructed in 1961 for the Frankfurt Auto Show. Reception was again not overwhelming, and plans to put the car into production were canceled. That was too bad, since this was the most attractive of all Type 3s and had four seats and a top that folded down out of sight. More than one may have been built, still to be discovered.

★★
**1968–1974
411 and 412 Sedan,
Fastback, and
Squareback**

Type 4
1968–1974

Early in 1963, Hermann Klaue, a Swiss engineer, hoping the job of chief of car design at VW would be his, submitted to Heinz Nordhoff detailed plans for a water-cooled 1,500-cc four-cylinder transverse front-wheel-drive unit to power the Beetle replacement. Nordhoff declined, and instead had Helmut Orlich develop the VW Type 4, known as the 411. It was Nordhoff's greatest mistake.

Putting this into perspective, it must be emphasized that Nordhoff was a great twentieth-century corporate leader. His accomplishments were legion. However, Nordhoff was not an automotive visionary, or perhaps his crystal ball was too clouded with past and continuing success. Like no other car since the Model T, the Beetle replacement was critical, and in some respects represented a no-win situation. But Nordhoff's refusal to accept the coming front-wheel-drive revolution caused problems at VW that took decades to recover from.

By the early 1960s, most European small-car manufacturers were beginning the conversion to front-wheel drive. Saab had been front-wheel drive since 1949, and in Great Britain, the Issigonis-designed Austin 7/Morris Mini 850 took the world by storm in 1959. Renault provided front-wheel drive for its unique R16 in 1965, and the smaller models fell in line, abandoning the rear-engine layout that had been in vogue since the end of World War II. Fiat's rear-engined 600 D eventually gave way to the 1968 Fiat 128, another front-wheel-drive transverse-engined layout. Peugeot followed suit with the 103 and 203 models. VW was being left alone in an increasingly competitive market. The 411 was on the European scene by late 1968, and imported to the United States in 1971. It was a brontosaurus surrounded by raptors.

Designated the Type 4, the 1971 model 411 poses next to the Super Beetle. The 411 was billed as the company's first four-door sedan, with nearly double the trunk space of the Beetle. All 411s had fuel injection.

Type 3 and Type 4 Comparison		
	Type 3 (Fastback)	Type 4 (Fastback)
Wheelbase	94.5 in	98.4 in
Length	166.3 in	179.2 in
Width	63.2 in	64.3 in
Height	58.1 in	58.4 in
Curb weight	2,010 lb	2,430 lb
Price	$2,454	$3,109

The 1973 model 412 fastback had higher taillights and front signal lights, a restyled nose, and 1,795 cc. Despite many standard features, the price was too high; $4,200 would have bought a new BMW in 1973.

The station wagon, or Variant, was a bit more pleasing to look at. Air conditioning was optional. The wagons outsold the fastbacks, but numbers were small in either case.

Although the new 411 was another completely new car, it retained the flat-four low fan engine from the 1600 series, but the capacity was increased to 1,679 cc with 85 horsepower. The upmarket philosophy established with the 1600 series applied again to the 411–that is, the car was designed to be even bigger, better, more powerful, and more expensive. As with the Type 3, which was still in production at the time, three models were offered: the fastback, the two-door sedan, and the station wagon, again called the Variant in Europe.

The chassis was a major breakthrough, featuring fully unitary construction, MacPherson front suspension, coil springs on all four wheels, and a fully double-jointed rear suspension on all models. Tires were usually 165srx15 Michelins. The VW three-speed automatic was standard, as was the Bosch fuel injection on all U.S.-spec models, and the four-speed manual was available. The Type 4 was tight, quiet, more powerful, and smoother than the Type 3, and equipped with full luxury accommodations including a gas heater. Luggage space was excellent–owing to the large, overhanging front end–with 8 cubic feet of space under a long, ungainly hood. The front springs were stiffer to accommodate the extra weight, and when unladen, the front end "sits high in the air and looks funny," commented *Road & Track*. Brakes, too, were a sore point, still having no servo-assist and requiring high pedal pressures.

The handling was also not up to 1970 standards. A sensitivity to side winds, which had been a VW trait; a longitudinal pitch over undulations; considerable body roll; and a poor turning radius were some of the objections. Worse yet, rust was even more serious on the 411 series than on the Type 3–which is why few of the Type 4s are still around today.

Perhaps the biggest turnoff was the looks. Patterned after the Renault 16, which was ugly as well but had a certain Gallic charm about it, the 411 was ill-proportioned and almost gruesome. The station wagon was the largest seller, perhaps because it was the most utilitarian.

In 1973, the 412 model was presented, with a remodeled nose and a 1,795-cc engine that produced less horsepower than the old 1,679-cc unit. The price for the station wagon was up to $4,200, but many features and options were standard, such as radial tires, a heated rear window, and an automatic transmission. Air conditioning was a $363 option.

The last of the line, the 1974 Type 4 model 412 wagon. Finding any Type 4 is difficult and questionable. But languishing in a garage somewhere out there is a mint-condition, low-mileage Type 4. It might be worth checking out.

The restyled front end did little to improve the looks of the 1973 model 412. Only 350,000 Type 4s were built, and production ended in 1974.

VW's ill-fated big car lived on to 1974, when production stopped after only 350,000 had been built. Tooling and production costs had been enormous, and the entire episode was a marketplace disaster at the worst possible time.

The 411 and 412 were VW's Edsel—and that's what makes them interesting cars today. No comprehensive VW collection would be complete without a Type 3 and a Type 4, but both are for serious collectors only. As transportation, a Super Beetle is more desirable; as a restoration project, the 411 will prove daunting to even the most eager. As with the Type 3, buy a Type 4 only if it is virtually mint, and pay the lowest possible dollar.

Chapter 13

K70 1970, Dasher (Passat) 1973–1981, and Fox 1987–1994

★ ★
1970 K70
★
1973–1981 Dasher (Passat)
★
1987–1993 Fox

How VW became an Audi dealer is an interesting story for both historian and owner.

Heinz Nordhoff died on April 12, 1968, leaving behind the Beetle legacy, but little future. When Kurt Lotz took control, he was faced with severe problems–such as the relative failure of the Type 3 and the definitive failure of the Type 4–and still no replacement for the Beetle. Lotz appointed Werner Holste technical director. Holste immediately began negotiations with NSU, a small German car company. NSU held the patents to the remarkable and advanced Wankel engine, which powered the front-wheel-drive NSU Ro 80 and a smaller, 1.7-liter four-cylinder version called the K70. By early 1969, NSU had become part of the VW family.

VW had already bought a majority share of the Audi firm. Audi was what was left of the pre-World War II German Auto Union combine, which then consisted of Audi, Horch, Wanderer, and DKW. (The four linked rings, still used as Audi's emblem, represent the merger of those four companies.) Audi re-emerged after the war and was purchased by Mercedes-Benz. A new, front-wheel-drive midsized car was designed by Mercedes engineers, but did not reach production until VW gained controlling interest in 1966. The new car, called the Audi 100 and 100LS, was successful, leading to a smaller version, called the Audi 80.

Lotz had much to choose from, and decided to market the NSU K70 as a VW for the 1970 model year. The K70 was never imported to

A lifesaver: Rudolf Leiding's VW Dasher, an Audi Fox with a hatchback. Not transverse-engined, it was still up-to-date enough to sell in considerable numbers from 1973–1982. It gave VW some much-needed time to develop an entirely new line of cars.

A Fox wagon was available in 1987, in two-door guise. The VW Fox, a reincarnated Audi Fox, now used the Golf 1.8-liter engine, although still mounted north-south, a legacy of the old Audi days.

the United States, but it was similar in concept and size to Audi's 80. The wheelbase was 96 inches and length 174 inches on the four-door model. The 1,700-cc overhead-cam engine produced 90 horsepower DIN with 102 foot-pounds of torque. As with the Audi, the engine arrangement was not transverse, but longitudinal.

Lotz also made the decision to utilize the Audi 80's 1.5-liter engine to power the next generation of cars. Time was running out, however. Market shares were falling, and an internal struggle was going on between Audi and VW. In September 1971, Lotz resigned and was replaced by Rudolf Leiding, then president of Audi. A battle that would shape the next 20 years had been fought and won.

Leiding wasted no time establishing the Audi 80 as the basis for the new VWs. Ludwig Kraus, who was the director of Audi engineering, became technical director, replacing Holste. The result of the revolution was the Audi Fox and the VW Dasher, which was called the Passat in Europe.

Little more was heard from the promising cars of NSU, and the daring Ro 80 had a short life span. Audi was now in control. In mid-1973, the Dasher started to roll off the production lines, just as the Type 3 production came to an end. The Dasher shared mechanical specifications with the Audi Fox, and both designs were from Italy's Giorgetto Giugiaro, but the VW was a fastback and, at 173.1 inches, some 10 inches longer than the Audi,

The curb weight for the Dasher was a light 2,110 pounds, benefiting from unit-body construction–which up to that time had been used only on the 411.

The Dasher's wheelbase was about 1 inch longer than the K70's 96 inches. The first Dasher engines were carburetor, rated at 75 horsepower from 1,471 cc, and available with a four-speed manual transmission. Tires were now 155x13s–making more room for a decreased turning radius. Suspension was the standard MacPherson strut, with coils and beam axle in the rear. Antiroll bars were standard on front and rear. Disc brakes in the front and drums in the rear were judged adequate. A two-door model could be purchased in 1974 for right around $4,000–a price that was not to last.

Dashers did not have a great reliability record, as owners cited problems with brakes, noise, instruments, emission controls, and interior controls. Still, the cars did what was expected of them, and in the *Road & Track* survey, 82 percent of the responding Dasher owners thought they would buy another. The old VW pride in craftsmanship and quality, however, simply wasn't there.

A two-door hatchback was offered in 1975, and in 1976, the troublesome carburetor was replaced with the Bosch K-Jetronic fuel injection. The displacement increased to 1,588 cc, and power to 77 horsepower. VW was hard at work making a go of the Dasher, and the 1977 models had a new interior and were much quieter than earlier cars. The 1979 four-door Dashers got the hatchback arrangement, and options included air conditioning, an AM/FM stereo, and a sunroof. Also in 1979, the Dasher diesel came on the market, equipped with the 1,471-cc Rabbit diesel powerplant. The VW five-speed manual was an option on both the gas and diesel models. Fuel consumption was excellent at 40 miles per gallon, but the price was not; diesels started at $7,818 in a market where no one cared much for them in the first place.

The Dasher era was about to close, after the cars of Leiding and Kraus had in fact helped save VW and provided affordable, modern transportation. But it was not really over yet; the Dasher was replaced by the larger Quantum in 1982, but even though the body was new, the old north-south engine layout and the engine itself were the same, a legacy of the Mercedes-Benz-designed Audi 100 of 1966.

A further legacy was the old Audi Fox, reincarnated as the VW fox in 1987. (Did you ever get a sense of déjà vu when seeing a new Fox? "Wait a minute . . . Haven't I seen this car somewhere before?") In a sense, the VW fox was a very different car, however. Giugiaro, who was entrusted with the original design, updated the interior and exterior trim. The engine was still not transversely mounted, but was a Golf 1.8-liter with 81 horsepower. The suspension was still MacPherson struts up front, but the rear axle was the VW profile torsion beam with trailing arms. All models, including the two-door station wagon, had a four-speed; no automatic or five-speed was available.

The base price was down, at $6,490, and this model filled the low end of the VW line-up. The five-speed transmission was made available in 1989, with the GL Sport trim package. The price was up to $8,115, still a deal for any German car. All VW Fox models were built in Brazil.

For 1993, VW upgraded the Fox to Wolfsburg Editions, and offered more than 40 standard features. Color-coded integrated bumpers and full wheel covers were part of the package, which also included 175/70 all-season radial tires, power front disc brakes, deluxe velour upholstery, map light, map pockets, child safety rear door locks, air conditioning, and a four-speaker radio.

The two-door version was called, almost confusingly, the Fox Polo, but the Fox was not related in any manner to the European-only Volkswagen Polo. The GL model was available only as a four-door. Colors for 1993 were Diamond White, Daytona Red, and Classic Black in nonmetallic, and Huron Blue, Moon Dust Silver, and Raspberry in metallic paint.

Rising Brazilian inflation kept the price of the Fox on an upward climb. Reliability was not up to par with the competition, and the design was a little long in the tooth. Thus, the very attractively packaged Fox/Polo was eliminated from the 1994 model year.

The 1989 Fox GL Sport with a five-speed transmission made a big difference in driving. All new VW Fox models were built in Brazil.

Chapter 14

Golf/Rabbit 1974–1984

★★
1974–1984
Rabbit

★★
1977–1984
Rabbit Diesel

★★★
1980–1993
Cabriolet

★★★
1980–1983
Pickup

★★★★
1983–1984 GTI

VW's new car was introduced with two names–the Rabbit, for U.S. customers, and Golf, for the rest of the world. We will use the name Rabbit for 1974–1984 models, after which the name Golf was used throughout the world.

The Rabbit was finally the worthy successor to the Beetle. But by 1974, 11 years after Hermann Klaue proposed a front-drive transverse-engine layout, after innumerable stopgap measures and in a vastly changed world, the Rabbit was almost an anticlimax. The Scirocco, introduced at the same time, stole much of its thunder with its sharp, attractive Giorgetto Giugiaro-designed coupe body.

The new Rabbit owed little to anyone, save the well-developed Audi 80 engine. Nor would the Rabbit share its unit body with any other corporate model. It was, however, indicative of a complete and comprehensive break with the past. The front-drive concept was now total and irrevocable; only the Transporter series would continue the rear-engine legacy. Type 3 production ended in 1973, Type 4 production ended in 1974, and by June 1974, the 1303 Super Beetle transferred production from Wolfsburg to Emden, Germany. No more Beetles would be produced at the factory created for the marque.

Despite initial doubts about the new Rabbit, it is now clear that it did indeed become the Beetle successor. The second-series Golf appeared in 1985, being similar to the Rabbit in style but nonetheless sporting a completely new body. The third series, more rounded and thoroughly modern, was introduced in the United States toward the end of 1992.

Early U.S.-built Rabbits had rectangular headlights and vertical side markers. By 1979, the Westmoreland plant in Pennsylvania was producing all the Rabbits for U.S. consumption.

This 1978 Rabbit C was among the last of the German Rabbits imported to the United States. Note the horizontal side markers. Pre-Westmoreland Rabbits sported round headlights and stiffer suspension.

From their introduction in 1974–1975, Rabbits had already built up an enthusiastic following in the United States. The softly suspended 1979 Westmoreland Rabbits did not sit well with U.S. buyers.

The basic Rabbit, ready for the European market in 1974, was a 146-inch-long two- or four-door sedan, with a transverse-mounted 1,093-cc or 1,471-cc engine (the Audi 80 engine) and a four-speed transmission. The wheelbase was 94.5 inches. The MacPherson front struts were aided by a unique independent suspension in the rear, with two trailing links and coil springs over tubular shocks, and a torsion beam connecting the two trailing links. Rack and pinion steering gave excellent response. The car's weight was only 1,720 pounds with a full 12-gallon tank of fuel. Deluxe versions had vinyl interiors and fully reclining seats. The entire package was attractively designed by Ital Design's Giugiaro. It was very much a car of the times.

For the U.S. market, the Rabbit suffered a 150-pound penalty for its U.S. Department of Transportation-mandated bumpers. One Zenith carburetor meant only 70 horsepower, but the three-speed automatic was optional. Also optional were radial tires and vacuum-assisted front disc brakes. The car had only one instrument dial, and it had rubber mats in the standard version. The list price was just under $3,000, or about $100 more than that of the Super Beetle.

The car was a winner. *Road & Track* tested it against eight competitive rivals including the Honda Civic, and found it far and away the best choice. The testers particularly enjoyed the handling, ride, and responsive steering–items the VW team had paid attention to in the design stage. The acceleration was by far the best in the group as well, as the quarter-mile was achieved in only 19 seconds, compared with the Honda's 20.4 seconds. Gas consumption was also better than most; *Road & Track* saw an easy 30 miles per gallon.

The engine of the 1979 C. Bosch fuel injection was standard from 1978 onward. Early drivability problems had been eliminated, largely owing to the more-efficient fuel injection that replaced the Zenith carburetor.

Further options included a Deluxe interior and comfort group and a Performance comfort and interior package. Carpets, adjustable seats, armrests, an inside hood release, and a locking glovebox were part of the interior package.

The Rabbit was not without problems, however. The 1974–1975 models had poor drivability, high noise levels, poor interior quality, and engine mount and alignment problems. For 1976, most of these problems were corrected.

The Bosch fuel injection was available in 1977, and a 1,588-cc engine was also offered, improving the drivability and acceleration. More significantly, the Rabbit diesel was introduced, becoming the gas mileage champion with an EPA rating of 52 miles per gallon highway and 37 miles per gallon town. VW figured around 50 percent of all Rabbits would be diesels–a situation that proved to be only temporary with the fickle American public.

The 1978 models were little changed. A slightly smaller engine of 1,457 cc was standard, however,

From 1980 to 1983, Westmoreland produced the VW pickup truck. This 1981 version had the optional topper. Most pickups were diesels, but gas engines were available. *Tim Parker*

This 1982 pickup was an LX model, with trim around the wheel arches. Script on the right side of the tailgate read "Diesel." *Tim Parker*

Note the rail on the bed of this 1982 pickup. The wheelbase of the pickup was almost 10 inches longer than that of the Rabbit, at 103.3 inches. Pickups are in much demand today in the United States; they were among the few front-wheel-only pickup truck models built. *Tim Parker*

The 1981 Rabbits were equipped with a larger, 1,715-cc engine. EPA restrictions wreaked havoc with car manufacturers during the 1980s. Adding to the piping was the optional air conditioning.

Rust makes itself known in unusual places: This on the A-pillar was apparently from wet foam in the framework. Thoroughly check out any Rabbit for the tin worm. *Tim Parker*

with the power down to 71 horsepower owing to emission requirements.

To accommodate the expected demand for the Rabbit and to help keep costs down, VW opened an assembly plant near Westmoreland, Pennsylvania, and by 1979, American Rabbits were rolling off the line. The 1979 Rabbits, as well as most of the rest of the VW line, were available with the five-speed transmission, which increased gas mileage and engine life. American Rabbits were recognizable for having rec-

tangular headlights, vertical side markers, and redesigned color-coded interiors. They were also heavier, and more softly sprung than the European Golf–leading to dismay among a growing number of Rabbit enthusiasts.

Another typical area of rust is in the engine compartment. Watch for Bondo, or other means used to cover rust, particularly around the shock towers. *Tim Parker*

Two model options were available: the C, for Custom, and the L, for luxury. The diesels were still selling well, particularly the five-speed. *Road & Track* was still impressed with the diesel after 100,000 miles, despite an engine rebuild, as overall costs were a mere $0.11 per mile.

For 1980, the standard engine was the 1,588-cc unit and the Rabbit convertible was introduced, as was the rare and now desirable Rabbit pickup, which was available with the 78-horsepower 1,588-cc gas or diesel and with a four-speed or five-speed manual or three-speed automatic. The pickup, also built in Westmoreland, was longer than the Rabbit, having a 103.3-inch wheelbase, as opposed to the Rabbit's 94.5 inches. Double-walled construction made the pickup extremely rigid, and the cargo box was low and flat, owing to the lack of a drivetrain. The Rabbit pickup, if found with the 1,588-cc five-speed, is the best Rabbit bet next to the Rabbit GTI for U.S. enthusiasts. The pickup disappeared from the U.S. model line-up in 1983, so examples are hard to find.

For the first few years of the Rabbit's life, it was consistently rated at the top of the small-sedan race. The price was creeping up yearly, however, and the competition from the aggressive Japanese was heating up. The 1981 models were equipped with an even-larger 1,715-cc engine, but still had only 74 horsepower. DOT and EPA regulation were making life difficult for all manufacturers during that era, and California had more stringent regulations, requiring a separate model for that state. The base price for a typical 1981 Rabbit was $6,920, and a ready-for-the-road version with a few options had a sticker price that was just under $8,000. The Rabbit S model appealed to those who had criticized the

A tale of two Rabbits: The early 1980s Rabbit S model was a pre-GTI car, built with stiffer suspension, and sport seats and trim. Power output, however, was standard. Note the smaller taillight arrangement. *Tim Parker*

The typical GTI treatment, with larger taillights, a wiper, and, of course, the GTI script in red. The 1983–1984 versions were rated at 90 horsepower. *Tim Parker*

Star-pattern GTI alloy wheels were another GTI visual hint, but wheel options abounded during the era. *Tim Parker*

The 1983 Wolfsburg Limited Edition Rabbit. Special wheels, paint, and interiors usually contributed to the Wolfsburg Edition cars. These would be nice to have, but few Wolfsburg Editions are particularly collectible.

By 1984, Rabbit GL interiors were becoming almost luxurious, definite improvements over the stark interiors of the 1970s.

soft Westmoreland Rabbit. It featured a stiffer suspension, sport seats, and trim, but had no more power.

By 1983, sales were plummeting, not helped by the recession, and the Westmoreland plant was not running up to capacity. Diesel sales fell sharply as gas supply worries decreased. The last bright spot of the Golf/Rabbit Series 1 was the GTI.

The origins of the GTI went back to 1975. High-performance small sedans had always been popular in Europe, with a tradition that originated with the Fiat Abarth 750s and Renault Gordinis. The German engineers got to work on the new Rabbit. GTI reportedly meant Gran Turismo, but no one ever figured out what the "I" meant; the logical assumption was that it stood for Injection, but that was never confirmed. The 1976 European GTI's were given a Bosch fuel-injected 1,588-cc engine with 110 horsepower. Uprated springs, and antiroll bar in the rear, and wider wheels gave the GTI the handling it needed to cope with the extra horsepower. Trim included a tachometer, sport seats, and a red-trimmed grille with a GTI label. The car was an immediate success.

The American GTI did not appear until 1983. Slotted into the engine compartment was a 1,780-cc powerplant modified to meet federal regulations for the new Golf. Wheels were cast-alloy 14x6 items from the Quantum, with 185/60 Pirelli P-6s. At 90 horsepower, the engine was well down from its European counterpart, but it had 16 more horsepower than standard U.S. Rabbits. The front suspension spring rate was increased 22 percent, the rear 29 percent, and stiffer front shocks were straight off the European Golf GTI. Antiroll bars were installed on both ends to minimize roll. The five-speed gearbox was tailored to the car with a final drive ratio of

3.94:1 versus the 3.89:1 in the standard Rabbit. Ventilated discs were provided in place of the standard solid discs. An interior trim package consisted of a new four-spoke wheel, sport seats, remote control mirrors, a golf-ball shift knob, and a rear window wiper. Externally, changes were few. A front air dam, flat-black trim, and red grille trim with GTI nameplates were subtle but important differences. Prices started around $8,500.

The handling was impeccable, nearly on par with that of the European GTI despite the car's being nearly 200 pounds heavier. Acceleration and performance were almost astounding: 0–60 miles per hour in 10.6

A 1984 line-up, with the GTI in the foreground. The L model is in the center, and the popular GL is at the rear. The GTI helped to bring up sagging sales.

seconds, 0-70 miles per hour in 14.6 seconds, and the quarter-mile in 17.7 seconds at 76 miles per hour.

Obviously, for potential buyers, this is the VW Rabbit to go for. Its years were numbered, as the 1985 model year saw the new Golf Series 2 intro-duced. The Rabbit GTI, so far ahead of its competi-tors and siblings, has already become a sought-after collectible. It is a happy end to the Rabbit line, which had saved VW from near bankruptcy.

Less happy was the closing of the Westmoreland plant, which had expanded to include the new Jetta. In the summer of 1988, almost 10 years after open-ing, the American experiment ended. Production of the Golf and GTI was transferred to Mexico, and of the Jetta to Germany.

Meanwhile, Karmann was busy producing the long-lived Golf/Rabbit Cabriolet. The new convert-ible was to replace the even longer-lived Beetle, and was introduced at Geneva in 1979. Karmann had al-ready built over 18,000 Cabriolets in 1978. The car arrived in the United States for the 1980 model year equipped with the 1,588-cc block, a three-way con-verter, and a lower compression ratio of 8.2:1.

The Golf/Rabbit was designed and engineered to be as light and rigid as possible. Karmann's task was to maintain the structural rigidity while not adding too much weight. Metal was added to the floorpan and around the front wheel arches; a box member was placed across the chassis just behind the rear seat; and finally, a sturdy Targo-type roll bar was installed. With the addition of a five-layer insulated top, the Cabriolet was almost 300 pounds heavier than the sedan.

Trunk space proved to be another problem, as Karmann's heavy-duty–and expensive-to-replace-top

The year 1984 was the last for the Rabbit. It had once been at the top of the heap, but by the mid-1980s, recession, the strengthened deutsche mark, and Japanese competition meant sluggish sales. The new Golf would be ready for 1985.

Introduced in 1979, the Rabbit-based convertible was very successful. This 1983 Wolfsburg Limited Edition illustrated why the car was so popular with college students, particularly young women. Convertibles were smart, were properly packaged, and had coordinated colors.

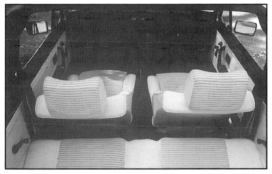

Karmann's convertibles had limited rear visibility because VW thought it important to retain the rear seat room, even while the top was down. Still, the 1983 Wolfsburg Edition had little room in back.

Well-proportioned from almost any angle, the convertible, particularly with the color-coordinated alloy wheels, was a striking car. Note the two round headlights.

was bulky when folded. The prototype model had the top stored neatly away in what was the Rabbit trunk. The lack of trunk space did not sit well with VW; therefore, the top ended up perched high on the rear deck, limiting rearward visibility. Like the Rabbit's, the rear seat can be folded forward to increase trunk capacity.

All of this did not limit sales, however, and by 1989, more than 100,000 had been sold stateside. Karmann had to do nothing when the new Golf was introduced in 1985; it just continued to produce the Cabriolet on the old Rabbit chassis. The Cabriolet continued to be popular with the college set, despite the 1993 price tag of just under $20,000.

The front seats of the 1984 Wolfsburg Limited Edition were both stylish and comfortable. Reinforcing sheet metal added almost 300 pounds to the total weight.

The GTI wheels on this 1985–1986 Cabriolet reminded one that the old GTI suspension was standard on the Karmanns. The Targa-type roll bar added to the chassis' rigidity.

New wheels, integrated bumpers, and dual headlights were seen on the 1989 Cabriolet. If you are shopping, find a late Cabriolet with a near-perfect top.

The 1985 Wolfsburg Limited Edition. It seemed that with each year, the interiors were a little wilder than the year before.

The Cabriolet has been on the market so long that it is now a living classic. The Cabriolet Classic of 1993 celebrated 37 consecutive years of VW convertibles and 14 years of the Rabbit-based Cabriolet. The 1993 models were powered by the 1.8-liter 94-horsepower four-cylinder.

The Golf-GTI suspension used on the Cabriolet was noteworthy, but despite the chassis modification, the Cabriolet did not handle as nicely as the GTI. Eventually, all three transmission options were available: the four- and five-speed manual and the automatic. The GTI package–virtually standard fare in the United States–included the 90-horsepower 1,780-cc fuel-injected engine, but performance also suffered in comparison, owing to the weight penalty. European versions ran the gamut from a 50-horsepower 1,100-cc engine to 110-horsepower 1,600-cc units.

The Rabbit-based Cabriolet, discontinued in 1993, was an unusual design. Certainly not pret-ty, it is nonetheless attractive with color-coded trim and interior packages, fender flares, air dams, and extended rocker panels. Rust does not seem to be a significant problem, although old leaky roofs will hasten the disappearance of the floor pan. The tops are extremely clever and well built and offer a heated glass rear window. But they are very expensive to repair or replace. Interiors, some with leather, tend to age rapidly in ultraviolet rays. A VW Cabriolet or pre-1985 Rabbit convertible can be an enjoyable experience or a money pit–so shop carefully, as you will find many to choose from.

Not too many changes were made for 1992, aside from the wheels, which offered many options and rocker molding. By 1989, more than 100,000 Cabriolets had been sold in the United States. Still based on the old Rabbit chassis, the Cabriolet continued into 1993–1994.

★★
1975–1980
Polo N, NL, LS
★★
1977–1980
Derby L, LS, GLS
★★
1980–1999
Polo C, CL, GL
★★
1980–1999
Classic Limosine
★★
1986–1999
Polo Diesel
★★★
1986–1999
Polo GT-G40
★★
1986–1999
Polo Classic
Coupe GT
★★
1995–1999
Polo, Classic,
and Estate

Polo 1975–1999

Amid the general confusion at Volkswagen in the 1970s, the question being asked was, "Will the real Beetle replacement please stand up?" Was it the K70, the Type 3, the Dasher, or the new Golf?

In March 1975, Volkswagen surprised the pundits with yet another new car, the Polo. With a wheelbase 2.5 inches shorter than the Golf and a 895-cc engine producing a familiar 40 horsepower, the Polo was perhaps the true successor to the famous Beetle.

However, comparisons should be made with the Golf rather than the old Beetle for as *Autocar* noted, "It is pointless to compare the Polo with the Beetle . . . they are so totally different, related by nothing but the Volkswagen name."

The Polo was similar to the Golf in that it had a front-wheel-drive transverse-mounted engine; unit-body, three-door hatchback construction; and MacPherson front suspension. The engine was a destroked Golf unit.

The rear suspension differed only in the placement of the torsion bar, which was a few inches rearward of the trailing arms, creating a rigid "H" pattern. Steering was rack and pinion. The four-speed transmission allowed a top speed of about 80 miles per hour and 0–60 miles per hour was achieved in 18 seconds, not bad for 895 cc.

The new Polo was aimed at Europe's minicar market, then dominated by the basic Mini 1000, the Hillman Imp, and the Fiat 127. None of these cars were imported to the United States, including the Polo. Two models were available initially, the N and L. The Luxury version offered front disc brakes (no servo-assist due to the car's light weight) and larger 135x13 tires. The Polo was Volkswagen's price leader in Europe, although very close to the bottom-line Golf. Polos were notable for their high-revving, oversquare engines and delightful handling characteristics. Radial tires, two-speed windshield wipers and washer, and heated rear windows were standard.

A third model was offered in September 1976, the LS. Displacement increased to 1,093 cc, which provided 25 percent more horsepower and 15 percent more torque. Tire size increased to 145x13, and the level of trim was suitably updated. The LS model put the Polo in the "Mini Supercar Class," with impressive acceleration of 0–60 miles per hour in about 16 seconds, and 50-70 miles per hour times 6 seconds quicker than the 895-cc model. Gas mileage remained high–both the N and LS were good for 30–36 miles per gallon. Competition was tough, however, as the larger engine meant the LS was pitted against the Honda Civic, Peugeot 104, Renault 5, and Ford Fiesta. The Polo fared well, but rarely received full points.

A 1986 Polo coupe, probably with the 1,100-cc engine. Never seen in the United States, the Polo was popular in Europe. Although Polos were excellent entry-level cars, VW had no plans to import the model to the States. *Tim Parker*

Three years prior to adding a trunk to the Golf to create the Jetta, Volkswagen applied the same concept to the Polo (though with less successful results). Called the Derby, the new three-box configuration increased the length from 11 feet 6 inches to 12 feet 8 inches and added 60 pounds to the overall weight. Trunk capacity was 18.2 cubic feet. Models included the L, LS, and GLS with a choice of 895 cc, 1,093 cc, or 1,272 cc in the GLS. Few opted for the 895-cc L model, primarily because 40 horsepower was inadequate for the heavier and larger Derby.

Equipped with the 1,272-cc unit, the GLS had the makings of a winner. With 60 horsepower available and weighing in at only 1,580 pounds dry, 0–60-miles-per-hour times decreased to 13.5 seconds, and top speed was in excess of 90 miles per hour. Overall appearance remained the same, but the GLS was more luxurious, even including a standard sunroof. *Autocar* summed up the LS and GLS as a "saloon derivative of the Polo Hatchback. Lively performance from a superbly smooth, free-revving engine. Controls are light and positive, with well-balanced handling with no excess understeer but heavy, rather dead brakes. All early Polos were carbureted, and like the early Golfs and Passats, drivability was often listed as a problem area. In the late 1970s, the term "Limousine" (why is beyond reason) was added to the Polo name in some markets.

By 1981, it was time to update the body. The most significant aspect of the new body was the extension of the hatchback to nearly the dimensions of a station wagon. The Polo's length was increased by 2 inches, and the width by 3/4 inch. Weight was up to 1,587 pounds, but the new body was very practical and had large areas of glass. Altogether it was a more pleasant-looking small car.

Polo, Golf, Beetle, and Dasher Comparison

Specs	Polo	Golf	Beetle 1200	Dasher/Passat
Wheelbase	92 in	94.5 in	94.5 in	97 in
Length	138 in	146.5 in	160 in	165 in
Width	61.5 in	63.5 in	61 in	63 in
Weight	1,510 lb	1,650 lb	1,670 lb	1,890 lb
Horsepower	40 hp	70 hp	34 hp	55 hp
Displacement	895 cc	1,093 cc	1,192 cc	1,296 cc
Tire Size	5.50x12	145x13	155x15	155x13

A Polo station wagon, 1986. With the right engine option, the Polo could have given Toyota Tercels and Honda Civics much-needed European competition in the United States. *Tim Parker*

Once again, three models were offered, the C, CL, and GL. The 895-cc option was replaced with a 1,043-cc engine, (also called the 1050) still producing 40 horsepower. The 1,093-cc, 50-horsepower model was not the midrange offering, as the 1,272-cc, 60-horsepower engine was available for both the Polo and the rebodied Derby. According to *Automobile Year*, "The addition of a trunk to the Polo to create the Derby was not one of VW's most successful marketing ploys, so the new Derby receives a body which owes nothing to any other model." The name Derby was soon dropped, and thereafter the three-boxer was called the "Classic" or the "Classic Limousine."

A fourth engine option was made available in 1986. The 1,272-cc Polo D used the diesel engine, rated at 45 horsepower. With the new five-speed gearbox, the D model easily topped 50 miles per gallon. Also new that year (introduced at the 1985 Frankfurt show) was the pocket rocket GT-G40. VW adapted the G-lader supercharger to the 1,272-cc engine, dropped it into the three-door coupe, and screamed to the top of the minicar genre. With fuel injection and supercharger, the G40's 115 horsepower propelled the little Polo to the top speed of 121 miles per hour and 0–60 in about 9 seconds.

Something to satisfy every market segment was the name of the game by 1989. On the low end was the 1,043-cc carbureted Polo with 44 horsepower, offered as a three-door sedan and coupe or a four-door sedan. The 1,272-cc (1300) "Classic" was available with either carburetion or fuel injection, depending on the market, and the 1300 Coupe GT offered 74 horsepower and a five-speed transmission. The GT-G40 found an enthusiastic audience, but was available only as a coupe. Lastly, the 1300 Diesel was still doing well. These choices were still available, essentially unchanged, into 1993.

In the 1990s the Polo concept was updated again, and it continued to be the Volkswagen low-cost product. The new Polo was very much in sync with the then-current designs from Honda and Toyota, more rounded and aerodynamic than its predecessor. The hatchback was referred to simply as the Polo, the notchback retained the Classic nomenclature, and the Estate was, as usual, Eurospeak for station wagon.

By 1998, the marketing reflected the need to conform to the new Euro III DM emissions, and the Polo was offered with a 1.7-liter, 60-horsepower injected diesel engine, as well as gas-powered powerplants ranging from a 50-horsepower, 1.0-liter to a four-valve 1.4-liter engine. A turbo diesel with 90 horsepower was an option with the Classic.

The GT-G40 concept was lost to the green movement, but the Polo is remarkably popular in Europe, particularly among the youth. Standard equipment included alloy wheels, four-wheel disc brakes, and ABS. Three option packages were available; the Sportline, Comfortline and Highline. The Highline was a comprehensive package that includes 6Jx14 "Indianapolis" wheels, sunroof, color-coded bumpers, front fog lights, and split rear seat.

Scirocco 1974–1988

★★★
1974–1988
Mark I and II
Eight-Valve
★★★★
1986–1988
16V

The Scirocco set the world standard for small, modern sport coupes. Introduced along with the Golf/Rabbit in 1974, it was immediately hailed by *Road and Track* as a "new and truly remarkable small GT."

Scirocco is the German spelling of the word *sirocco*, which is a wind on the North African coast. The car was to be renamed Blizzard for the American market but good sense prevailed, and the Scirocco kept its original moniker for both continents.

Also like the Golf/Rabbit, the European version had an optional 1,093-cc engine of VW design. The 1,471-cc version was available with 70 horsepower or 85 horsepower, and the models were listed as the L, LS, and TS. Suspension and mechanicals were identical to those of the Golf/Rabbit.

The new Scirocco was designed as a replacement for the long-running Karmann-Ghia, and like the Ghia, was assembled by the Karmann factory. The design was pure Giorgetto Giugiaro, making the most of the then-current wedge-and-folded-paper idiom. It offered a lot of space for

A remarkable car in 1974, the Rabbit-based Scirocco. This was the early Euro version with rectangular headlights. Giorgetto Giugiaro was responsible for the design, which held up well through the years.

SCIROCCO

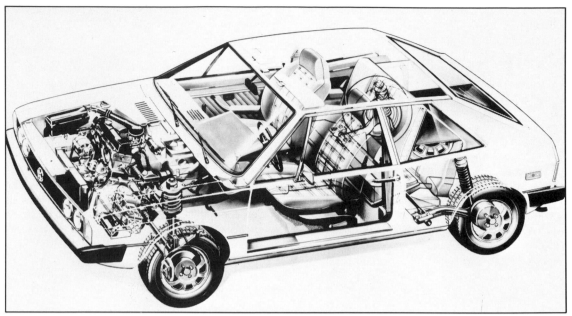

The chassis was pure Rabbit, but fortunately, that too was another good design. The U.S. version had a 70-horsepower 1,471-cc engine with a single Zenith carburetor.

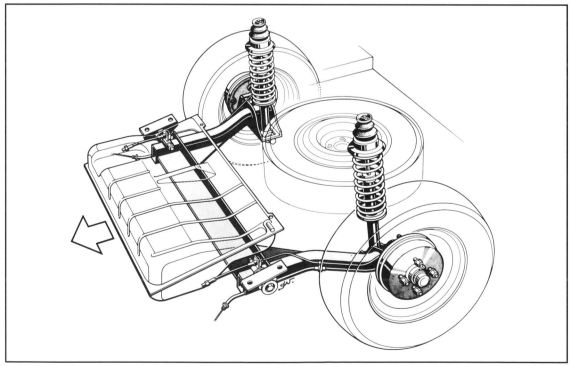

The rear suspension was a pressed-steel beam with an integral stabilizer bar and coil springs over shocks; it was simple, effective, and inexpensive.

its tight parameters; the Scirocco had the same wheelbase as the Golf. It was advertised as a 2+2, so the rear seats were marginal, but for two passengers, the luggage space was plentiful, including the trunk's 8.2 cubic feet of space under the hatchback.

In the United States, only one model was offered, called simply the Scirocco. For 1974 and 1975, the 1,471-cc U.S. engine with Zenith carburetion was good for 70 horsepower. Acceleration was good, 0–60 miles per hour in 12.7 seconds, and the quarter-mile was finished off in 19.4 seconds. A few options were offered–including alloy wheels, which were a "mandatory" option at $140–for list price of $4,672. The three-spoke lightened steering wheel was attractive, but the seats were somewhat loud; one wit claimed that the seats must have left clowns without their trousers all over Germany.

The formula was a success, so few things were changed for 1976, but the engine was increased in size from 1,471 cc to 1,555 cc, and a single wind-shield wiper took the place of the previous two. The Bosch fuel injection was available in 1977 to aid the drivability problems. Gone too was the clown interi-or–and the seats were now almost infinitely adjustable–but gone as well were the standard vent windows. Gas consumption, always a strong point with both the Rabbit and the Scirocco, remained at 30 miles per gallon.

Owners still had problems with cold starts, rust, and imprecise shifting linkage. Many of the troubles associated with early Rabbits plagued Scirocco owners as well. But the car improved with each year.

More improvements came with the 1979–1980 model year, with the optional five-speed transmission–the 1,588-cc engine now good for 76 horsepow-er–and the air conditioning option. The car was a good 90 pounds heavier now, and with the air, the performance was hardly up to 1977 specs. But whatever else might have suffered, the five-speed option improved the capabilities of any VW and is perhaps the

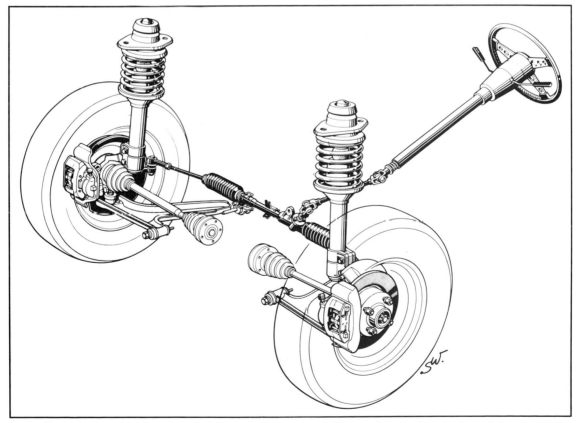

Front discs were standard, rack and pinion steering meant 3.25 turns from lock to lock, and the suspension offered beefy lower A-arms with MacPherson struts.

Aluminum-alloy wheels were a "mandatory option," but 1976 models were provided the 1,555-cc engine, still carbureted. Early Sciroccos tend to rust, just about everywhere.

most desirable option to consider. A limited-edition model with Recaro seats was on tap, but the total package now came to $8,710, almost double the original price in 1974. The 1979 limited-edition package provided the basis for the 1980 Scirocco S, complete with a Kamei-built air dam and 5x13-inch alloy wheels with 175/70 tires. The S was the U.S. version of the European Storm, unfortunately without the leather seats and colors available on the Storm. The S model carried out the last year of the first series of Sciroccos.

Mark I Sciroccos are already finding an enthusiastic following. Rust seems habitual, but mechanically,

The 1978 Scirocco. A single windshield wiper replaced duals in 1976; the 1977 model used Bosch fuel injection; and signal lights were getting larger. The bumpers were slightly improved over the older battering rams.

the cars are easy to restore and parts are readily available. A truly fun car, with a remarkable history, the Mark I is an excellent buy, provided a relatively rust-free example is obtained.

Giugiaro's crisp lines and wedge shapes were not liked by all, as attractive as they might be. In 1980, a new design was submitted by VW's Herbert Schafer, who did an excellent job of smoothing out Giugiaro's original design. The Mark II, or Series 2, was, if anything, more attractive, and well balanced. The drag coefficient was lower, the nose was better aerodynamically and had better crash resistance, and a functional spoiler in the rear was responsible for a 60 percent reduction of rear lift. The length was increased 6.5 inches, but other dimensions remained unchanged.

Introduced at the 1981 Geneva show, the new Scirocco came to the United States in 1982 with a 1,715-cc engine that was new, although very similar to the older Audi-based 1,588-cc block. Horsepower was still 74 at 5,000 rpm, but the car managed again to top the competition in most respects, The base

The 1981 S model did not have leather seats, as the European Storm did. We were back to a rather bold interior design. A five-speed was optional from late 1979 on.

By 1981, the original Scirocco—dubbed the replacement for the Karmann-Ghia—was ready for a restyling. Raised white lettering on this 1981 does little for the car. This is the S model, the U.S. equivalent of the European Storm.

price was now up to $10,000, considerably more than that of the car's rivals.

The 1983 Scirocco benefited from an even larger, 1,780-cc engine, with 90 horsepower. But it was losing ground to the Honda Preludes and Toyota Celicas, and costing more as well. The price with a sunroof and metallic paint could run well over $11,000. The interior trim, with a new pod-style dashboard and elegant seats, was in the best German tradition, with the feel and atmosphere of true quality.

Performance was on par for a sports coupe, and excellent even by today's standards. Still making use of the single-over-head-cam four-cylinder two-valve design, the Scirocco was good for 110 miles per hour, did 0–60 miles per hour in 10.7 seconds, and had an all-around gas consumption rate of a frugal 27 miles per gallon. It was a fine and well-developed model, and the designers had little left to do but provide trim packages.

For Karmann fans, the 1983 Wolfsburg Edition had a Karmann badge and special GTX wheels. Many of the 1984 Sciroccos were also equipped as Wolfsburg Limited Edition models, with black B-pillars, multifinned 14x6-inch Passat wheels, and a rear spoiler. The 1985 version was virtually unchanged. But the end of an era was at hand.

Up to the early 1980s, despite the EPA requirements that demanded improvements such as catalytic converters, smog pumps, electronic ignition, and fuel injection systems, it was still possible for the average car enthusiast to tune and maintain

In-house designer Herbert Schafer modernized the Giorgetto Giugiaro Scirocco, and came up with the Mk II. Design changes were much more than visual: The Mk IIs had a lower drag coefficient and better crash resistance.

The increased glass area of the 1982 Mk II was obvious. The Mk II was longer by some 6.5 inches. The bumpers, however, still left something to be desired.

a vehicle. But an increasing number of cars built after 1985, particularly those of interest to the enthusiast, became so complex as to render the average owner virtually helpless. Supercharging, turbocharging, or multivalve layouts with double-overhead camshafts became the accepted norm. Engine compartments were so heavily burdened with hardware, both mechanical and electronic, that it became a project simply to change plugs—about the only thing an owner *could* do without expert help. Gone were the days of the Beetle engine, which could be removed in less than a hour and repaired by most anyone who could read.

For this reason, the buyer must beware. The high-performance small sedans of the 1980s are available today at reasonable prices, but maintenance and repair may cost more than the owner is willing to handle. In most states, emission control requirements for 1980–1990 vehicles are tight and getting more stringent, making frequent tune-ups and even overhauls a necessity. Ironically, by the mid-1980s, most auto manufacturers, including VW, dramatically reduced the rust problems prevalent in earlier cars. Therefore, what money might once have been set aside for rust repair must now be saved for mechanical upkeep, which in most cases must be done by either the dealer or a competent shop.

The interior design department undoubtedly had its way with the Scirocco and the Cabriolet. Both, of course, were from Karmann. The 1984 Wolfsburg Limited Edition Scirocco was, again, luxurious.

VW met the technological revolution of the 1980s head on with the Scirocco 16V with its 16-valve engine. Introduced in Europe in 1985, it did not reach the United States until mid-1986. VW engineers and sales staff were impressed with the tremendous success of the Golf GTI, yet faced increasing competition from Japanese automakers,

Herbert Schafer's interior was more pleasing as well, but still bold. The dashboard, however, remained strictly Teutonic.

The 1985 Wolfsburg Edition was somewhat tarted up, with a Karmann badge, spoilers, and finned 14x6-inch wheels, but the same old single-overhead-cam, two-valve engine limited performance.

The cure for performance woes was the introduction of the 16V engine in 1986. This increased the horsepower from 90 to 133 in the U.S. version, making the Mk II capable of doing 0–60 miles per hour in 7.7 seconds.

The last of the line in the United States. The 1988 Scirocco interior was a bit more subdued, attractive, and, as usual for VW, ergonomically correct.

Ford, and Opel. The old Audi-based four cylinder had been developed to its full potential, and more power was needed. More cubes were not the answer. Tax laws and a desire for low gas consumption kept most European engines under 2.0 liters. VW confined turbocharging, with its related heat problems and acceleration lag, to diesel applications. Supercharging had potential but was not yet at the stage where it could be marketed. That left the multivalve, multicam solution, which had already been developed by German speed merchants such as Oettinger.

At the 1984 Frankfurt show, VW introduced its unique 16V head, still based on the 1.8-liter four-cylinder block. Production was delayed while the engine was made reliable and at the same time cost-effective to produce. In its final form, the 16V was a narrow double-overhead-cam design, with sodium-filled 28-millimeter exhaust valves arranged almost in line with the block, and 32-millimeter intake valves placed 25 degrees to the right. A larger, improved timing belt drove the exhaust cam, and the intake cam was driven on the opposite end of the engine with a simple chain attached to the exhaust cam. Inverted hydraulic buckets were activated by the camshaft, which was placed slightly off center to allow the buckets to rotate. Pistons were cooled by an additional steam of oil sprayed underneath toward the piston head, a feature automatically activated after the oil pressure dropped to 28 pounds. The oil was cooled by surrounding the oil filter with water.

The new Bosch KE fuel injection system replaced the old K, and with knock sensors, Lambda sensors, and a catalytic converter, the 16V was ready for the U.S. market. It offered 33 horsepower more than the old eight-valver, for a total of 123 horsepower. European versions did better, as usual, with 129 horsepower, and 139 horsepower for the non-catalytic model. Torque was 123 foot-pounds at 4,200 rpm, and 118 foot-pounds at 3,800 rpm for the U.S. version.

Even the U.S. model was fast–faster than a Porsche 944 or Mazda RX-7. The Scirocco 16Vs did 0–60 miles per hour in 7.7 seconds, and fin-

The best was probably the last, the 1988 Scirocco 16V. Body-colored bumpers (red, black, and silver) and lower body side skirts meant 16V. Note the rear-mounted radio antenna.

ished the quarter-mile in 16 seconds. They were demonstrably faster than the competition, and handling was even better than before, owing to shorter, stiffer springs; a larger rear antisway bar; and 185-60HR-14 tires, still on 6-inch alloys. Discs replaced the drums in the rear, and up front, large ventilated discs were standard.

Scirocco 16V models sported body-colored bumpers, front and rear spoilers, and lower bodyside skirts, and were offered only in red, black, and silver. The radio antenna was placed on the back of the roof, angled toward the rear of the car.

The standard single overhead cam was still available, but VW expected that more than a third of the Sciroccos sold would be 16Vs. Sales were not strong, but Sciroccos were available until 1998.

Of all the Sciroccos, the 1986–1988 16V is the hands-down winner in the best bet category, already sought after and sure to be a future classic. But remember, these are complex cars, needing the best of care and equipment to maintain them.

Chapter 17

Syncro, Quantum, Vanagon, and Golf 1986–1989

★★★
**1986–1988
Syncro Quantum**
★★★★
**1986–1989
Syncro Vanagon**
★★★★
**1986–1999
Syncro Golf**

The engine of the Rallye Golf. Equipped with the G60 supercharger, the Rallye golf also had the Syncro four-wheel-drive package. The G60 supercharger can be seen just forward of and under the alternator.

The story of the Syncro models is another short but interesting chapter in VW history. (The lack of the *h* in the name is not only intentional, but trademarked by VW.) Again, Audi provided the lead and incentive for the four-wheel drive program.

A number of technological advances and a competitive rallying series in Europe made the use of four-wheel drive more cost-effective and at the same time more popular. The advent of front-wheel drive, pioneered by Citroën and adapted by the British, changed the rally world, as British Motor Corporation's Mini-Coopers dominated the rally scene in the 1960s. During the same period, the Ferguson company in Britain was developing a fluid viscous drive for four-wheel drive application.

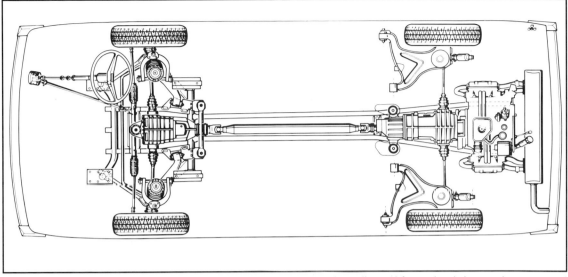

Four-wheel drive, as featured on the Vanagon. The viscous coupling allowed four-wheel drive to be engaged automatically for optimum traction.

Ferguson installed it in a number of race cars, including a Grand Prix contender. Entering the rally scene with gusto, Audi created the legendary four-wheel-drive Audi Quattro, which dominated the international rallies much as the Mini had 20 years earlier. This, in turn, led other European manufacturers to jump on the bandwagon, developing four-wheel-drive sedans for rally use.

In the United States, interest was increasing in four-wheeling, both off-road and in severe weather conditions. Jeeps and Wagoneers were selling far too well for the likes of Ford and General Motors, which brought to market their own version of all-wheel-drive vehicles. The trend was clear. In 1988, certain models of Pontiac, Subaru, Toyota, Audi, VW, and BMW all could be ordered with four-wheel drive.

And a trend it was. Like turbocharging, fins, and muscle cars, the four-wheel drive phenomenon was temporary, at least in terms of demand. By the dawn of the 1990s, few sedan manufacturers were still offering a four-wheel drive option, at least in the United States—although the four-wheel-drive truck market remained strong.

VW, with easy access to Audi technology, jumped in with all four wheels. In 1986, the company was indicating that soon four-wheel drive would

Skid plates and longitudinal runners added to the weight of the Syncro Vanagon. The total weight was now over 4,000 pounds.

The 1986 Vanagon Syncro, camper variety, had an increased ride height. Syncros came with a 2.1-liter, 95-horsepower flat-four to try to offset the increased weight.

be available on every model, including the Golf, Jetta, Vanagon, and Quantum.

It was easy to adapt existing Audi-based models to four-wheel drive, so VW concentrated on re-engineering the Golf for all-wheel drive. The Golf Syncro turned heads at the 1985 Frankfurt show and was by far the most exciting of VW's four-wheel adventures.

The interior was almost identical to that of the standard Vanagon, but note the four-wheel pattern in the center of the dashboard.

A 90-degree power takeoff was placed right between the front halfshafts and connected to a drive shaft. This led to a unit that appeared to be a transaxle but was the housing for a Ferguson-patented viscous coupling. A rear differential then sent the power to the rear wheels, connected by a full independent suspension, with single lower A-arms and coil shock struts. The first models were eight-valve engines, but the 16V was to be the powerplant of choice, particularly for the U.S. market.

What made the Ferguson patent different from most other four-wheel drive applications was the fluid drive. Within the housing, muliplate clutches were placed between the driveshaft and the differential. The clutches were encased in the silicone fluid, which when idle was thin and "loose." Under normal driving conditions, the front and rear wheels rotated at the same speed, thus creating an "idle" condition for the fluid, and drive was provided only to the front wheels. If, however, the front wheels started to spin six percent faster than the rear, the fluid became heated and "tight," allowing the driveshaft to begin to propel the rear wheels. This was done automatically, and it evenly distributed the power between the front and rear wheels.

The Golf Syncro was introduced with rally championships in mind. The Golf Rallye was a Syncro produced in Belgium specifically to meet the homologation requirements: 5,000 models were built in 1989 to meet these guidelines. The often-changing rules of the rally game frequently frustrated VW and prevented it from achieving the successes of Audi, but the Golf Rallye production was sold–to Europeans only–immediately. the standard version, using the G60 supercharged engine, had a top speed of over 130 miles per hour and did 0–60 miles per hour in 7.6 seconds.

Another version of the Golf Syncro appeared in 1989, and was called the Montana. Later called the Country, this prototype was designed for serious off-road use rather than competition rallying. The Country had ample ground clearance, a protective sump grille, and kangaroo bumpers.

Much to the regret of Americans, none of the Golf Syncro models were ever imported to the United States, as had once been planned. Priorities were shifted to adapt the four-wheel drive concept to more versatile cars–notably the Quantum station wagon and Vanagon, two four-wheel-drive VWs that can be found in the United States.

In 1986, the Ferguson system also found its way onto the Vanagon Syncro. A drive shaft was taken forward from the transaxle to the Ferguson-equipped differential for the front wheels. All road tests had similar comments regarding the transfer arrangement, giving high marks for the smoothness of the operation. "The transmission of torque to the front wheels is continuously and infinitely variable, and the delivery is so smooth that occupants are generally unaware of anything except nonstop motive traction," said the often-critical *Car and Driver* magazine.

Further traction aids were made available. A stump-puller low gear could be engaged, and a switch activated a servo that locked up the rear differential. It was hard to get stuck in a Vanagon Syncro.

The servo system, along with protective chassis skid shields, added 330 pounds to an already overweight Vanagon, now tipping the scales at over 4,000 pounds. To offset this, Vanagon Syncros came to the United States with a 2.1-liter 95-horsepower flat-four and Digifant fuel injection. In fully equipped Westfalia

A 1986 GL Syncro. GL Syncros were a little lighter than the fully equipped campers and offered better performance.

Quantum Syncro, U.S. style. Introduced in 1986, the Quantum was among a number of midsized cars to incorporate four-wheel drive. Syncro script was on the right side of the tailgate.

The 1987 GL Syncro. Quantum Syncro interiors offered the same luxury as their two-wheel-drive siblings. The anticipated popularity of four-wheel drive did not pan out, and by 1990, Syncros were no longer available.

form, the Syncro was a little slow, doing the quarter-mile in somewhat over 20 seconds. However, the standard GL model was also available, with four-wheel drive, offering better performance but less luxury.

Adapting an Audi-based Quantum chassis to four-wheel drive was much easier and less costly. Audi was not using the Ferguson viscous drive, but installing a full-time locking differential arrangement, with a locking option for either the central or rear differential unit. Four-wheel drive is fine unless just one of the wheels starts spinning, and that's when the locking differential is called into play—manually, of course, by the driver. This system, developed on the original Quattro in 1981, was installed on the Audi 4000 in 1984 and its sibling Quantum in 1986.

For the United States, the Syncro option was available only with the station wagon. There was no particular reason for this, but as sales of the Audi Quattro in the United States were downright dismal.

110

A slightly higher ride height and full trim options made the Quantum Syncro easy to identify. The Syncro feature disappeared with the coming of the Passat.

VW sought to appeal to the Aspen, Colorado, types–either those who lived there or those who aspired to live there. It was priced accordingly, at over $3,000 more than a similar equipped Quantum GL5 sedan. (Trends tend to be pricey.)

The five-cylinder was updated to 2,226 cc and put out 15 horsepower more than the two-wheel-manual transmission was the only choice in gearboxes. Fuel economy suffered a bit, being down to 19 miles per gallon. VW's Quantum Syncro was a good car, but not a great four-wheeler, and did not fare well in comparison with the competition.

VW Syncros are almost an aberration. The Golf Rallye will become a classic. The Vanagon Syncro is interesting but not exciting, and the Quantum is difficult to call. Advantages are low numbers and rarity, but four-wheel-drive systems can be troublesome and costly.

The Syncro line disappeared with the coming of the Passat. The Vanagon Syncro did not sell well, and by 1991, it was hard to buy a new Syncro of any type in the United States. The 1993 line for the United States did not include any four-wheel drives.

Chapter 18

★★
**1982–1988
Quantum**

Quantum 1982–1988

VW's Dasher was neither a great car nor a sales leader. But in the course of a 10-year life, it had provided VW buyers with a vehicle that was a little larger and more useful than the Super Beetle or Rabbit. An even larger, more luxurious version was planned for the early 1980s. At last, VW would have the upmarket car Heinz Nordhoff had unsuccessfully tried to create.

The Dasher was called the Passat in Europe, and both were based on the Audi 80, called the Audi Fox in the United States. In 1980, a new Passat was introduced in Europe and was followed shortly by a range of models, slightly larger, under the name of Santana. This variation of the Passat theme was imported to the United States in 1982 as the Quantum, replacing the Dasher. VW liked the Quantum name, assuming most customers would associate it with advance nuclear physics and high technology. Nothing new appeared under the hood. The trusty 1,715-cc single-overhead-cam unit placed north-south was aided by the five-speed transmission–which VW called Formula E, for Economy–and the three-speed automatic was optional. The Bosch K-Jetronic injection was standard. To aid drivers, an upshaft indicator light was placed between the tachometer and speedometer, blinking when an upshaft was most efficient for fuel economy. Apparently it worked; early Quantums were good for 29 miles per gallon.

The chassis was based on tried-and-true principles as well, using the MacPherson front struts with VWs, but the beam rear axle of the Dasher was replaced by the torsional trailing arm suspension from the Rabbit

Between the Dasher and the Passat came the Quantum. This is the rare Quantum coupe, 1982 style. Over-priced by about $3,000, the Quantum aimed at the BMW-Mercedes market.

The Quantum wagon was well made and attractive, and used the same suspension layout as the Golf. Early Quantums could achieve 29 miles per gallon.

and Scirocco. Brakes were rated excellent, provided the optional 6-inch alloy wheels with 60 Series tires were on the car. The power steering fell short of normal VW standards, with poor feedback and return-to-center. Performance, with the 1,715-cc engine, was not dramatic, but adequate: 0–60 miles per hour in 13 seconds and the quarter-mile in 19 seconds flat.

What made the Quantum particularly attractive, however, was the high quality of the interior. VW tried to emulate Mercedes, with excellent carpeting throughout and a high grade of plastic and vinyl, although unlike Mercedes, the Quantums used a tweed-like cloth material for the seats. The

tachometer and speedometer on the coupe, and clock and speedometer on the wagon, were well placed and easy-to-read. Many small compartments situated strategically were great for maps, coins, gloves, or flashlights. Visibility on all models was outstanding, owing to the low beltline and slim A- and B-pillars.

The price was again on the high side. A coupe equipped with alloy wheels, sunroof, air conditioning, and AM/FM radio was listed at $12,500. The

Quantum and Dasher Comparison

	Quantum	Dasher
Wheelbase	100.4 in	97.2 in
Length	178.1 in	173.1 in
Width	66.2 in	63.6 in
Curb weight	2,505 lb	2,160 lb

Even 1982 models sported upmarket interiors. All materials were of high quality, with a tweed-like cloth for the seats.

The 1983 sedan was offered with both the five-cylinder Audi engine and the turbo diesel, which was EPA-rated at 41 miles per gallon city and 50 miles per gallon highway.

Initially, only the station wagon and the coupe were available in the United States. In 1983, the four-door came in with an additional package: the Audi five-cylinder engine. This gave the Quantum the performance it had lacked, but unfortunately was not available with the attractive coupe. The Audi five was a 2,144-cc single-overhead-cam good for an even 100 horsepower, or 25 horsepower more than the four. It enabled the new Quantum to take a second off its 0–60-miles-per-hour time and its elapsed quarter-mile time. It was the largest engine VW had ever marketed in the United States, and the fuel economy suffered; if you find a Quantum five, it will return only around 20 miles per gallon, on the average. Along with the large engine came a larger price tag: a four-door GLS cost $13,980.

The year 1983 was also the year of the turbo diesel. VW's 1.6-liter diesel was uprated by the installation of a turbocharger, and in this guise, it gave 68 horsepower with 98 foot-pounds of torque at 2,800 rpm. With the five-speed gearbox, the Quantum turbo diesel nearly matched the performance of the gas-powered 1,715-cc four, but the gas mileage was EPA rated at 41 miles per gallon city and 50 miles per gallon highway. The old four-cylinder

competition, largely from Japan, was logging in at around $3,000 less. Sales were adequate, however, and helped by the fact that in 1983 the United States was just coming out of a recession and about to experience a boom economy. The Quantum not only stayed the course, but was continually upgraded.

The dash layout of the 1986 Quantum was par for VW during the mid-1980s. The interior rated high marks in contemporary road tests; steering did not.

diesel was modified to take the additional boost of the turbocharger, including heat-treated exhaust valves, new wrist pins and cylinder head bolts, and a high-capacity lubrication system.

Few changes in the Quantum occurred until the addition of the Syncro in 1986. The third generation was on its way, and this time, models on both sides of the Atlantic would be called the Passat.

The Quantum was relatively short-lived. VW was now on a path to further separate itself from Audi-based products. Furthermore, something new and modern was needed if VW hoped to compete in a very tough market segment. The answer to both of these issues was provided by VW's technical director, Ernst Falia. His new transverse-engined VW Passat replaced the Quantum in 1989.

The 1987 GL sedan sported GTI-like wheels and rectangular lights. Quantums were neither exciting nor inexpensive, and sales were slow.

The 1988 GL5 was a decent car, and perhaps overlooked. The Quantum was replaced by the Passat in 1989–1990.

Chapter 19

★★
**1981–1984
Jetta, Diesel,
Turbo Diesel**

★★
1983–1984 GL

★★★
1983–1984 GLI

★★
**1985–1992
Jetta, GL**

★★
**1985–1992
Jetta Diesel**

★★★
**1985–1992
Carat, GLI**

★★★★
1988–1992 GLI 16V

Jetta 1980–1992

For being simply a Golf/Rabbit with a trunk, the Jetta was a most re-markable car. The addition of a few more cubic feet of space in the form of a third box transformed the hatchback into a seemingly larger, more luxurious Euro sedan. The trunk added 15 inches to the overall length of the Rabbit; all other specs were identical to those of the Golf. It was a stroke of genius on the part of the marketing people, who fore-saw the demand for the traditional three-box shape; the designers, who gracefully adapted the Golf; and the engineers, who managed to retain the handling qualities of the hatchback while adding the refinement and formality of a sedan.

Introduced in 1980, the Jetta was a success on both sides of the At-lantic. Updated with the Golf in 1984, its lines became smoother and more pleasant. The GLI and GLI 16V were true performance sedans at the top of their class. The bread-and-butter diesels and GLs are good buys, and the GLI and 16V models will be eagerly sought-after in the not-too-distant future. It is hard not to like the Jetta.

The basic Jetta used the 76-horsepower 1,588-cc fuel-injected en-gine from the Rabbit, and transmission options were the three-speed au-tomatic or the standard five-speed manual. Acceleration was better than that of most of the direct competitors, although VW maintained that the Jetta was a potential threat to the BMW 320ii. Suspension was also Rab-bit, and the early Jetta's ride was noted to be a bit stiff, a logical result of the car's stiffer springs and shocks.

The first Jettas were based on the Rabbit body, and were more angular than 1985 and up models. The addition of a trunk trans-formed the Rabbit.

Setting the Jetta apart from the Rabbit was a better-quality interior, with velour standard and leatherette a $60 option. Sill-to-sill carpets were color-coordinated, and the overall finish was excellent. Metallic paint and a sunroof were also early options. At the time of introduction, a new Jetta could be had for right around $8,000.

Of course, the Jetta came only as a four-door sedan, right? Wrong. A two-door model was available through the early 1990s. The numbers must be small, however, as I cannot recall having ever seen one on the road.

Engine options and trim packages later added to the choices of Jetta models: the diesel, the turbo diesel, the GL trim package on the four-door model only, and in 1984, the GLI. All were good cars. The GLI was an exceptional car, and the old version was only made for about a year before the new Golf-based Jetta came onto the market.

The GLI was simply the four-door Jetta version of the best-selling Rabbit GTI. Almost every good piece of the GTI became part of the GLI: the full GTI suspension, including 14x6 alloy wheels shod with 60 Series Pirelli P-6 radials; the tuned 90-horsepower 1,780-cc GTI engine; the interior package, with sport seats, steering wheel, tachometer, and extra console instruments; fenders flares; blacked-out trim; and in this case, a red GLI emblem. The GLI also came with almost the same performance–0–60 miles per hour in 11.2 seconds, the quarter-mile in 18 seconds, and a top speed of 112 miles per hour; in other words, it was just a tad slower than the GTI, owing to the 180-pound weight penalty added by the trunk.

The 1984 Jetta GLI was Rabbit-like but had comfortable seats. It was to get much better.

Air conditioning and AM/FM stereo cassette options drove the price of the Jetta GLI to new highs at more than $10,000. Now, the car was legitimately compared to the BMW, and the price, though high, was half that of the 318I. Like the GTI, the GLI family supercar was an instant best seller.

In 1985 came the controversial new Golf body and, with it, the updated Jetta. This shell was controversial because many thought it was not different enough from the old one, and wondered why VW should go through the cost of an entirely new car if most people had great difficulty determining the old from the new. It was, however, a more obvious

The 1985 Jetta was based on the new Golf. The higher trunk line increased space and improved lines.

The larger trunk area can be seen from this view of the 1985 GLI. Improvements drove the price up to near-ly $13,000.

change on the Jetta, as the trunk was raised for more space and better aerodynamics. The effect was a bet-ter-looking Jetta. Headlights were now single rectan-gular units rather than smaller quads; the grille was smaller; and the rain gutters became recessed strips in the roofline.

The interior was upgraded with the 1985 models, but all mid-1980s VWs seemed to share the same steering wheel.

The Jetta II was longer than the old model by an-other 4.8 inches, most of this being in the longer wheelbase it shared with the new Golf. Interiors were revised with better heating controls, and a larger body meant more interior space in the cabin. The Carat, a luxury version without the performance options, was a new model that continued until 1993. The GL and GLI were continued with the new chassis. Notable for the new chassis was the addition of disc brakes in the rear, with ventilated discs up front. Engines offered in the United States in 1985 were the 1.6-liter diesel with 52 horsepower; the turbo diesel with 68 horse-power; the 1.8-liter 1,780-cc four with 85 horsepow-er; and the GLI option, rated at 100 horsepower, ver-sus the previous 90 horsepower in the Series 1 GLI.

The Jetta II was a better car all the way around–and with the new model, the option list grew. A power group that included electric windows, mirrors, and central locking set one back $595, pow-er-assisted steering another $265, cruise control $200, and a ski rack $75. In no time at all, the un-der-10-grand Jetta was closing on $13,000. But in comparison with the BMW and the Mercedes 190, it was, a bargain.

VW wasn't done yet. For the United States, the years 1988–1993 were a high spot on the perfor-

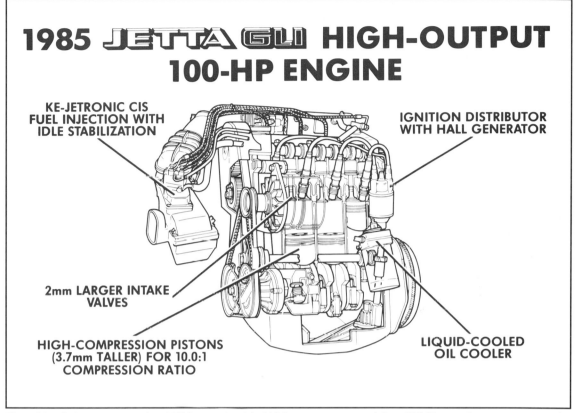

1985 JETTA GLI HIGH-OUTPUT 100-HP ENGINE

KE-JETRONIC CIS FUEL INJECTION WITH IDLE STABILIZATION

IGNITION DISTRIBUTOR WITH HALL GENERATOR

2mm LARGER INTAKE VALVES

HIGH-COMPRESSION PISTONS (3.7mm TALLER) FOR 10.0:1 COMPRESSION RATIO

LIQUID-COOLED OIL COOLER

The 1985 GLI engine was the 1,780-cc unit with 100 horsepower, providing GTI-like performance. Note the liquid oil cooler.

mance chart for VW buyers. This short but illustrious era will not be forgotten. The 2.0-liter double-overhead-cam 16V engine was inserted into the GLI in 1988 and remained a popular choice until its untimely demise in 1993. Of all the Jettas through 1993, the GLI 16V was the best Jetta yet—and perhaps ever—and is the best bet, despite the daunting complexities of its powerplant.

By 1988, the GLI was a well-developed medium-performance sedan. Taking the 123-horsepower 16V straight from the GTI-Scirocco made the Jetta "a true sports sedan that likes to get physical," according to *Road & Track*. The 16V was the old GLI but better, described as having "spirited performance, balanced, predictable handling marked by power on the understeer and moderate, trailing oversteer, respectable braking, user-friendly interior with great ergonomics, proper instruments, anatomically correct leather wrapped

Rear seat room and a large trunk make the Jetta a popular family car, designed to compete with the BMW and Mercedes-Benz low-end sedans.

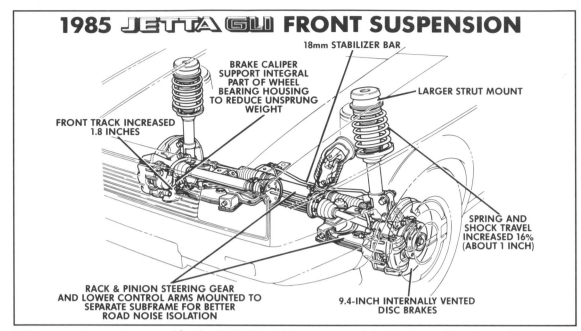

1985 JETTA GLI FRONT SUSPENSION

18mm STABILIZER BAR

BRAKE CALIPER
SUPPORT INTEGRAL
PART OF WHEEL
BEARING HOUSING
TO REDUCE UNSPRUNG
WEIGHT

LARGER STRUT MOUNT

FRONT TRACK INCREASED
1.8 INCHES

SPRING AND
SHOCK TRAVEL
INCREASED 16%
(ABOUT 1 INCH)

RACK & PINION STEERING GEAR
AND LOWER CONTROL ARMS MOUNTED TO
SEPARATE SUBFRAME FOR BETTER
ROAD NOISE ISOLATION

9.4-INCH INTERNALLY VENTED
DISC BRAKES

VW's suspension was improved for the 1985 GLI, with larger, vented disc brakes and a wider track. Discs were now standard at the rear as well.

The Wolfsburg Limited Edition in 1986 included a rear spoiler and special wheels, interior, and paint.

steering wheel, comfortable, gripping Recaro front seats . . ." as *Road & Track's* testers went on and on. Stiffer springs and retuned suspension made the GLI even better in the slalom than the older GLI.

But it was the 16V engine that really made the difference. Perhaps a bit fussy under 3,000 rpm, the unit pulled smoothly to the 7,200-rpm redline, doing 0–60 miles per hour in 8.8 seconds, 1.6 seconds faster than the old 100-horsepower two-valve GLI. The quarter-mile was shorter as well, with the new 16V making the distance in only 16.6 seconds. A continuing lower dollar also meant the new Jetta was up in price, now listing at over $16,000, with most options tacked on.

VW had come a long way from the Beetle, but the effort to convince buyers that here was a BMW in all but name was difficult. Just as the 16V began to hit the showrooms, the economy went into recession. Sales plummeted. But Volkswagen was about to give the Jetta a new lease on life.

Left
The 16V four found its way into the Jetta in late 1987, and transformed the car. Finally a true performance sedan, the GLI 16V was the best bet among all early Jettas yet built.

120

The dashboard layout of the 1987 16V reflected performance as well. The power group included electric windows, central locking, and electric mirrors.

Further upgrading the interior, VW installed Recaro seats in the 16V sedan–a fitting complement for the outstanding performance allowed by 123 horsepower.

The ultimate four-cylinder Jetta. The 1989 Wolfsburg Limited Edition 16V left nothing wanting. Note the red GLI on the grille.

A 1991 model with normal GL specs, with the 1.8-liter 100-horsepower engine. The 16V was still an option.

Chapter 20

★★
1985–1992 Golf

★★
**1985–1992
Golf Diesel**

★★★
1985–1992 GTI

★★★★
**1987–1992
GTI 16V**

Golf
1985–1992

At first glance, it is difficult to differentiate the earlier Golfs from later Rabbits. It takes a trained eye. The effect was purely intentional, but created controversy both in the United States and in Europe. Nonetheless, the design lasted until 1993, when the new-generation Golf was unveiled. Despite the comments from the press, the decision as well as the design was sound.

VW's new baby, now called Golf all over the world, was a bigger and better car. The wheelbase was 2.9 inches longer than that of the old Rabbit; the total length was increased by 3 inches, 4.7 inches, or 6.8 inches, depending on whose figures one believes and what bumper types were used; and the width was increased by 2 inches. The seating space was increased front and rear, and the luggage compartment size was increased by 42 percent. Another significant improvement was the drag coefficient, reduced from 0.42 to 0.34. All of this was accomplished without adding more weight.

Very few parts were interchangeable with those from the older model. The engine size, 1,788 cc, was close to that of the Golf/Rabbit GTI 1,780-cc, but the unit was in fact a different one with bigger valves. The new version put out around 85 horsepower, very close to the power of the GTI. This gave the standard Golf performance on par with that of the old GTI. Suspension changes occurred front and rear. The MacPherson struts featured a bushing that allowed more compliance, while reducing toe-in, toe-out movements under braking and acceleration. At the rear, the Quantum V torsion bar was adopted. These improvements

The 1985 Golf was most easily identified by the hatchback and taillight arrangement. It was a completely new chassis and body, but the similarity to the Rabbit created controversy.

made the Golf just as quick, or quicker, through slalom tests. Brakes for the standard version retained the front disc, rear drum arrangements, but overall, the only item that didn't improve was the gas consumption, dropping from an overall 29 miles per gallon from the GTI to 26 miles per gallon for the Golf.

Air conditioning and heaters were far better on the Golfs–lessons learned from the American market. The Westmoreland cars did not differ from their German counterparts, aside from DOT and EPA modifications. U.S. VW fans would have very little to complain about. The base price was just under $7,000, and options included air conditioning at $650, an AM/FM stereo cassette player, power-assisted steering, a rear window wiper, full wheel covers, and handy but clumsy fold-down rear seats. Like the Rabbit, the Golf could be had with three or five doors, and it maintained rectangular headlights, versus the round quad units of the European versions.

The next step was including more luxury options, and the GL, as it was known, was popular in the United States. The GTI model featured the 102-horsepower 1,780-cc two-valve engine, obtaining the

Interiors were dramatically updated, and finally, the four-buttoned steering wheel was gone. More cloth, less vinyl was the key.

extra horses by virtue of a revised camshaft, higher compression, and modified fuel injection. It was equipped with the familiar GTI trim and logo, now applied to the new body. But for the first time, the GTI had four-wheel disc brakes.

Trick rear seats–carried over from the Rabbit–make the hatchback more versatile. Improved quality was obvious.

The standard Golf interior, 1985, was functional and strait-laced. The first Golfs had the 85-horsepower 1,781-cc engine, but performance was close to that of the old 90-horsepower GTI.

The rear of the 1986 GTI. GTI script was located just under the right rear taillight. By now, GTIs were not the pocket rockets of the past. The GTI 16V fixed that.

The year 1987 was the year of the Golf GTI 16V, which was only available as a three-door. Given the brake update from the GTI two-valve and the improvements made to the basic 1,780-cc block, the GTI stood ready to accept the 16V head. The GTI was lowered by .05 inch, and the wheels were 14x6 aluminum-alloy with 205/55VR P600 Pirellis. The 16V, first introduced on the second-series Scirocco, was good for 123 horsepower in the U.S. version. The five-speed gearbox, however, was short on the final drive ratios, meaning that at 60 miles per hour, the engine was already revving at almost 3,300 rpm.

Acceleration was again the GTI's strong suit. It did the quarter-mile in 16.5 seconds, or roughly 0.5 second faster than the much-touted Acura Integra RS. The 0–60-miles-per-hour dash was achieved in only 8.5 seconds. Handling was again superlative, as the suspension, always good, was fined-tuned over the years of development.

The 1986 GTI. With somewhat different star-pattern wheels, the new GTI had a 103-horsepower two-valve engine and rear disc brakes.

This was the pocket rocket of the mid-1980s: the 123-horsepower 16V engine mounted in the GTI. The 1987 16V engines used the 1,780-cc block, and the technology had been developed by European speed merchants.

The 16V in contrast to the normal 1987 two-valve engine. The two-valve engines were at least easier to maintain, despite the plumbing, whereas the advanced multivalve engines made tasks like changing the head gasket formidable, to say the least.

Four years of Golf offered only minor improvements. The vent windows were gone and side molding was enhanced, but overall, few changes appeared for 1989.

Another style of wheels for the 1989 Golf Wolfsburg Edition. A rear window wiper was an option, as were power steering, air, and an AM/FM stereo cassette.

This kind of performance seemed to satisfy the buyers, at least for a few years. In 1990–1991, the Passat-based 1,984-cc block was given the full 16V treatment and placed rather quietly into the Golf GTI.

This combination produced 134 horsepower, and the Golf GTI, for a brief and shining moment, was the undisputed winner of the small-sedan performance stakes. Finally, the United States had a car with speed and performance equal to those of European models. In the long line of the Golf/Rabbit models, this is the one to search for.

For 1990, Golfs received a minor face-lift, and the 1.8-liter two-valve was uprated to 100 horsepower for the standard and GL models. The line continued without major changes, waiting for the third-series Golf, ready in Europe in 1992 and in the United States in 1993. However, the days of the high-performance Golf sedan in the United States were ending.

Germany and other European countries continued to get even-faster Golfs. Most notable was the G60. With 160 horsepower under the hood, the G60 could top 135 miles per hour. The G60 supercharger was applied to the normal eight-valve head, and it didn't take long before VW Motorsports adapted the G60 to the 16V head. According to Ian Kuah in his book *VW Power and Style*, 70 Golf G60 16Vs were produced by the Brussels, Belgium, plant, making it the "fastest production road car to have left any VW plant destined for a private customer." The G60 16V, although in full compliance with U.S. emissions regulations, was not shipped to the United States.

For the more practical, Volkswagen was about to bring to the U.S. a new generation of Golf. The emphasis was not on performance, but ecology.

This may be the ultimate U.S. Golf: The 1990 Wolfsburg Limited Edition GTI 16V. The full 2.0-liter engine was set up with the 16V head and produced 134 horsepower. This is the best bet for Golf enthusiasts.

Chapter 21

★★★★
1990–1991 G60

★★★★
1992–1995
SLC VR6

The Corrado featured exciting new looks, and performance. This is a 1992 G60, one of the last of the four-cylinders. Corrados were based on the Golf chassis, with appropriate modifications.

Corrado 1990–1995

The Corrado brought about two major technical developments. One was the G60 Lader, or G-shaped supercharger. The other was the VR6, which was to serve as the basis for the Golf III GTI and Jetta VR6.

Gone are the days of the Beetle, when an increase of 5 to 10 horsepower over a 15-year period was sufficient. Today, we seem to be almost frantically searching for increased horsepower, with the two restraints of reasonable fuel economy and low emissions. These are worthy goals, no doubt, that make for exciting automobiles. From the pacesetting Rabbit GTI of the early 1980s, with a whopping 90 horsepower, to the 178-horsepower stock and standard Sports Luxury Coupe (SLC) VR6, VW has come a long way in a very short time.

As was fitting for a technical showpiece, the Corrado, introduced in Europe in 1988 and the United States in late 1989, could be purchased with the 16V engine in Europe only, with the SLC VR6, encompassing all three of the high-tech engines from VW.

The 16V powerplant was the same one used on the Jetta. The G60 Lader had an equally interesting story, which began in 1905 with the patent of a spiral supercharger by a Frenchman named L. Creux. Air can

The Corrado came to the U.S. market in late 1989, for the 1990 model year, equipped with the G60 Lader. This model will be a rare one, as it was quickly superseded by the VR6. The supercharger was located below the alternator.

A European Corrado VR6, 1992. With 178 horsepower on tap, the Corrado VR6 could do the quarter-mile in less than 16 seconds, with a top speed of around 140 miles per hour.

be compressed in a number of ways–the Roots system, radial flow, and the eccentric vane being several used for enhancing the power on the internal-combustion engine. Creux's idea was to send air through a series of spirals, then compress it with a spiral-shaped impeller. The spiral and housing created a G-shape, thus G-Lader, or supercharger. VW's engineers rediscovered the patent in the 1970s, and started to improve on the idea using modern materials. By the late 1980s, the problems, primarily dealing with production, had been solved, and a smaller G40 supercharger was fitted to the Polo.

VW's slide-rule set was never completely happy with turbocharging, but it worked well enough with diesels. Turbocharging creates turbo lag, while the supercharger, driven directly off the engine, provides instant power throughout the rpm range. On the downside, supercharging also eats up horsepower, while the turbo gets its drive from the exhaust, with minimal loss of power. The search for a better way to gain smoother horsepower with vastly increased torque resulted in a resurgence of supercharging.

A larger supercharger was designed for the 1,781-cc single-overhead-cam eight-valve engine and called the G60. The torque advantage was tremendous. The G60 was rated at 166 foot-pounds of torque at 3,800 rpm–compared with the normal 120 foot-pounds at a higher 4,250 rpm. Horsepower went from 123 to 150, despite the loss of almost 18 horsepower to drive the supercharger. The induction process was complex. Air was taken in by the Digifant fuel injection metering unit, went into the G-Lader, passed through an intercooler (because compressed air gets hot, and hot air means less density and a propensity for pre-ignition), was then properly cooled, and advanced to the inlet manifold.

The Corrado was a worthy replacement for the Scirocco–although production of the Scirocco continued for European markets. Herbert Schafer was responsible for the design, with the rounded lines a further departure from the knife-edge school popularized by Italy's Giorgetto Giugiaro. Aerodynamically, the Corrado was excellent, as verified by a drag coefficient of only 0.32. A further aerodynamic aid was the

Designed for a transverse front-wheel-drive application, the narrow-angle VR6 fitted nicely into the Corrado engine compartment. By early 1993, the VR6 was only available in the Passat and Corrado in the United States.

The 1993 Corrado was available with either a five-speed manual or an electronically controlled four-speed automatic, complete with sport or economy modes.

automatic rear spoiler, which rose at about 45 miles per hour and returned to normal position at 25 miles per hour. Overall, the Corrado had a classical shape that harked back to the old Ferrari 275 GTB/4, and the classic shape is appreciated by enthusiasts. VW called the Corrado a sports car, rather than a GT. It must be recalled that VW was heavily involved in the design and production of two of Porsche's sports cars, the 914 and 924.

Based on the Golf floorpan, the Corrado used the standard GTI 16V MacPherson struts and the latest Passat trailing arm rear suspension, which provided passive rear wheel steering. The interior was similar to that of the latest Passat, and that is a warm compliment. As was the Scirocco, the Corrado was a limited 2+2 with ample luggage space. But it was bigger than the car it replaced: 2 inches longer, with a wheelbase 3 inches longer, and 1.6 inches wider. The wheels and brakes were suitably updated, with 15x6 aluminum-alloy wheels and 185/55VR radials, and 10-inch ventilated discs up front and 9-inch solid discs in the rear. A five-speed gearbox was standard.

The G60 was the only engine offered when the Corrado was introduced in the United States. To accommodate the supercharger, the head was heat-treated, the exhaust valves were sodium-filled, and the pistons were cast with larger wrist pins. The performance was on par with that of the Porsche 924s.

The car did 0–60 miles per hour in less than 8 seconds and had a top speed of 137 miles per hour. But the Corrado, at around $20,000, was far less expensive than its rivals.

One would think the G60 would be enough for at least a few years. But with a weight penalty of some 400 pounds more than the Golf, the Corrado was due for some good old cubic inches. Enter the VR6.

A bit of history first. A long time ago and very far away, an Italian genius by the name of Vincenzo Lancia realized the virtues of compact V-layout engines, and proceeded to design narrow-angle V-8s, and V-4s, for his 1920s and 1930s Lancias. In 1937, Lancia designed a 1,352-cc 18-degree V-4 with staggered pistons, steel liners, and an alloy block, mated to a single head with a single overhead camshaft. The car destined for this engine was called the Lancia Aprilia, and it set new standards in almost every category of design.

It is a bit of a folly, then, to hail VW's 2.8-liter 15-degree V-6 as a "revolutionary, breakthrough design," as some magazines have done. The only major difference from Lancia's design was the inclusion of two cylinders, an additional belt-driven overhead camshaft, and, of course, motronic fuel injection. From the staggered pistons to the aluminum-alloy mono-head, the new engine was a shining monument to the genius of Lancia. VW saw it as a way to get more cylinders in a transverse layout. This was not a bad idea, but certainly not a new one.

Having given credit where credit is due, I will add that the VR6 was still an exciting new engine from competent engineers. That it powered the

The new interior featured an optional CD changer control, an antitheft alarm system, central locking, chlorofluorocarbon-free air conditioning, a tilt wheel, and a multifunction trip meter, to name a few options. It was a true luxury sports coupe.

flagship of the fleet was no surprise. The Corrado with the new VR6 offered some 178 horsepower but, more significantly, 177 foot-pounds of torque at 4,200 rpm. This was great power, but as *Motor Trend* pointed out, very hard for the front wheels to handle. Torque steer took on a whole new meaning. The 0–60 miles per hour could now be achieved in much less than 7 seconds, and this was the first take of the engine. Top speed was somewhere over 140 miles per hour.

The last Corrado was a mighty attractive package. Optional equipment included an electric tilt sunroof, heated seats and heated windshield washer nozzles, leather-faced seats, cruise control, a central locking system, and antitheft alarms. Standard equipment meant an ABS for those huge four-wheel disc brakes. The VR6 carried on the rounded Schafer body. The grille had been revised, as had the front spoiler, but the visual changes were almost unnoticeable. The price was still a bit under $25,000–a considerable deal for the power and style. Good things don't always last. In 1995, with the introduction of the GTI VR6, the Corrado was no longer offered in the U.S., leaving a hard-core group of Corrado enthusiasts more than a little upset.

Chapter 22

Passat 1989–1997

★★★
**1989–1993
Passat 16V**

★★★
**1994–1997
Passat VR6**

★★
**1995–1996
Passat GLS**

★★
**1997–1997
Passat TDI**

The end of the Quantum meant the beginning of the Passat. Ernst Falia's new design, based on the existing Quantum platform, turned the engine around to a transverse layout, and VW dropped the Audi five-cylinder engine used in the Quantum. The new layout not only allowed a fresh architecture, but increased legroom within the same overall length. The wheelbase was extended to 103.3 inches from the Quantum. The front end treatment was a dramatic change, as the hood now came down to the bumpers and no traditional grille was evident. Air intakes were provided in the front air dam, and the new Passat was aerodynamically more efficient than the boxy Quantum.

European buyers could opt for the 1.6-liter turbo diesel, a 1.6-liter carb version, a 1.8-liter fuel- unit with 90 or 107 horsepower, and a 2.0-liter 16-valve four with Bosch K-Motronic injection and 136 horsepower (DIN). The Passat arrived in the United States with only one engine option, the 2.0-liter 16V four rated at 134 horsepower. The five-speed transmission was standard, and a four-speed automatic optional.

Although the unit body was entirely new, the MacPherson front strut and torsional trailing arm suspension from the Quantum were retained, as handling had never been a problem with the Quantum and continued to be a major strength with the Passat.

Four-wheel disc brakes, front ventilated, were now standard, and the Teves ABS was available as an option.

Ernst Falia, VW technical director, turned the engine around 90 degrees and used the 2.0-liter 16V four to power the new Passat in the United States. Although based on the old Quantum, it was virtually a new car.

The shape of the 1990s: The new Passat was aerodynamically much improved over that of the old Quantum, and yet retained the suspension that worked so well on the Quantum.

The station wagon tradition continued with the 1993 Passat, with its rounder form. Options included an electric sunroof with an air deflector and cruise control.

Rear view of the 1993 Passat GLX. The X will indicate the VR6 engine in all new VWs. A new Passat in this form could top 130 miles per hour and do 0–60 miles per hour in 7.9 seconds.

Performance for the 1990 five-speed sedan was the best ever: 0-60 in 8.8 seconds and a top speed of 127 miles per hour. EPA-rated gas consumption was rated at 21 miles per gallon city and 30 miles per gallon highway.

In 1990, the Corrado was just coming into dealer's showrooms, therefore a coupe version of the Passat seemed redundant. The four-door sedan and station wagon were the only Passat models available. As befits a luxurious German car, the interior appointments included soft leather upholstery as an option. Options included an electric sunroof with an air deflector, an alarm system, heated front seats, a six-speaker AM/FM stereo, cruise control, power windows and a central door locking system. Ten colors were available.

VW's upmarket car was coming of age. As good as the Passat was, it was ready for a new engine, and the VR6 was brought on board for the 1993 model year. Although the 2.0-liter 16V was still available, the flagship was the GLX VR6 sedan with a leather interior and moonroof. The VR6 gave the Passat the smooth, effortless performance expected of a luxury sedan.

The VR6 met with widespread approval, and in 1994 was the only engine available in both the Passat

Attractive 15-inch BBS wheels were shod with 215/50-15 all-season radials. ABS was included in the GLX package, plus an electronic traction control system that helped prevent wheel spin.

sedan and station wagon, and the only package was the GLX, which offered just about any option made. Both models were now covered by a truly comprehensive warranty package that included a 10-year 100,000-mile powertrain warranty available to the original purchaser. A 100,000, 10-year body rust through warranty was supported by a complimentary scheduled maintenance for two years or 24,000 miles.

By 1995 the Passat was right in the middle of one of the most heavily contested market segments in the U.S., and was up against the Honda Accord, Ford Contour, Chrysler Cirrus, Mazda 626, and Toyota Camry, all V-6 powered. Falia's engineering concept proved most competitive, however. Although the sales figures never matched Honda's or Toyota's, the Passat offered a unique, driver-oriented midsized car that virtually matched the benchmarking Honda. In a very telling *Road & Track* comparison test, the Passat was judged as better handling than the competition and, overall, was

The luxurious but standard velour interior of the 1993 GLX. The dashboard and side panels would be redesigned several times during the model's lifespan.

The GLX Passat interior for 1993 lacked nothing. The seats were multi adjustable, and the factory provided compact disc (CD) changer control capability, a tilt steering wheel, cruise control, dual remote heated mirrors, and so forth. (Remember that 1938 VW dashboard?)

1993 Passats had rather flat alloy wheels. The early Passats featured the distinctive front end treatment. Air was fed into ducts in the airdam below the bumper. This is the GL, with the 16-valve 2.0-liter four.

The 1994 GLX sedan. Note the 15-inch six-spoke BBS wheels, available only on the GLX. The Passat was developing into a contender in the midsize sedan class, but sales never reflected the Passat's overall excellence.

The GLX became the Passat bestseller, and by 1994 was available with the VR6. Note the spoiler, part of the GLX trim package, which also included fog lamps and body-color mirror housings.

For 1995, the Passat was given a grille that blended harmoniously into the overall design. Lights and signal indicators were also new. This is the GLX Wagon.

Like its sedan counterpart, the wagon was a clean, nicely integrated design. The GLX was the only trim option available in the 1995 model year. Station wagon prices started at $21,320.

Passat's new look for 1995 included a redesigned trunk on the sedan, incorporating the spoiler into the sheet metal as a slight lip. As the GLX was the only trim option available, the VR6 was the only, and the best, engine option.

A 1996 GLS Passat. VW again offered the four-cylinder option for 1996, but without the four-valve head. All Passat models were built in Emden, Germany.

rated third, behind the Honda and Mazda 626. Price, too, was right on the mark at $22,930 fully loaded.

One of the more distinctive features of the original Passat, the long hood and faceless front sheet metal, disappeared on the 1995 models. The Passat now had a grille, which brought it into line with the rest of the VW products. Honda was to do much the same thing with the Accord at about the same time, and neither effort was for the better.

Ergonomics were improved for the 1995 model year, with redesigned door handles, switches, and an optically improved instrument panel with easy-to-read gauges. New standard features were heated power mirrors, a multifunction trip computer, and a one-touch power window system that enabled the owner to open or close windows outside the car by inserting the key in the door.

It was one step forward, and at least one step back for Passat in 1996, as VW re-introduced the 2.0-liter engine for the United States under the lower-

priced GLS banner. This time the four didn't even feature the 16-valve head, but was a two-valver with an output of 115 horsepower, almost 20 less than the GLS of 1993. The GLX was still the flagship with the VR6, but VW touted the GLS as "the lowest-priced European midsize sold in the United States." Concentrating on updating safety specs to 1997 standards, the Passat range offered daytime running lights, adjustable shoulder-height safety belts, automatic locking retractors for child seats, and improved side-impact protection.

Now nearing its 10th year in the United States, the Passat had established itself as a viable contender in the midsize sedan market, and the GLX had proved to be a fine car from any perspective. Still, sales were low. Only 10,467 Passats had been sold in the U.S. by mid 1996, far less than Honda or Ford midsized sedans. VW was in the throes of an identity crisis, received very little press, and the *Fahrvergnugen* ad campaign was a dismal failure. As

1997 was the last year of Falia's Passat, and this is the rare but probably unjustly ignored diesel version of the station wagon. The TDI on the grille means Turbo Direct Injection. It was able to achieve 47 miles per gallon.

a leading VW spokesman described the malaise, "The worse thing that can happen to a car company is that nobody cares. We were gone in the minds of the public and the media."

VW continued to make hasty marketing decisions as well. In 1997, the last year for the Falia design, the GLS four cylinder was *again* dropped, this time in favor of–a diesel. Aside from Mercedes, diesels have never sold well in the U.S. market, despite the increased gas mileage. Gas prices in the U.S. were the lowest in years, and SUVs, never known for fuel economy, were all the rage. Nonetheless, the 1.9-liter TDI (Turbo Direct Injection) diesel with 90

horsepower was installed in the Passat TDI. It did have a wonderfully flat torque curve, peaking at 149 foot-pounds at 1,900 rpm. Torque-laden, the TDI also got an EPA mileage rating of 47 highway and 38 city, great for a midsize sedan. And it could be driven from New York to Chicago on one tank of diesel fuel, all while meeting both European and U.S. emissions. The secret was in the design of the head, which used direct fuel injection rather than ignition in a separate combustion prechamber. But, of course, the Passat diesel was short-lived. VW was again to reinvent the Passat, and the 1998 model would be once again based on an Audi chassis.

Chapter 23

Jetta III
1993–1999

★★
1993–1999
Jetta GL

★★
1993–1999
Jetta GLS

★★★
1993–1999
Jetta GLX VR6

★★
1996- 1999
Jetta Trek,
K2, Jazz

★★
1998- 1999
Jetta TDI

In 1991, for the third time, VW once again did the trunk act with the totally new Jetta, based, of course, on the totally new Golf III. In Europe, the Jetta was now called the Vento and, like the Golf III and EuroVan, had been on the road for almost two years before making an appearance in the United States.

The Jetta shared the same chassis as the Golf but with an additional 14 inches in length to accommodate the trunk. The softer, more aerodynamic lines of the Jetta III were nicely blended to accommodate the extra bulk and were most pleasant to the eye. Quieter and more luxurious than the old Jetta, the basic model came to the U.S. with the same 115-horsepower 2.0-liter four as the Golf. Interior room was also increased from the old model, and a simply huge trunk offered 15 cubic feet without dropping the rear seat forward. That doubled the space available.

The new engine provided a more usable torque curve due to the new cross-flow head. The 16-valve was no longer available in the United States, but VW was quick to introduce the Jetta VR6 GLX, which got off the ground for the 1994 model year.

The new 2.0 engine was fed by a Bosch Motronic fuel injection system, and helped the Jetta to achieve 23 miles per gallon in the city and 31 miles per gallon on the open road. The new body, with a CD rating of 0.32, was also improved over the old Jetta. If you didn't like to shift gears, the four-speed automatic was available on all models.

The all-new 1993 Jetta III GL was based on the equally new Golf. The 2.0-liter engine now put out 115 horsepower, 15 percent more than the old powerplant.

Introduced in 1993, the Jetta III didn't get rolling until 1994, and by 1995 the line-up already included the VR6 in the GLX package. The car was an instant winner, topping all comers in a critical *Road & Track* comparison test.

1995 Jetta GL was based on the Golf III platform, but smoothly blended the third box into the overall design. The GL model, with a growing list of standard features and available options, was a constant in a constantly changing model line-up.

For 1994, VW offered three versions of the Jetta in the U.S.; the basic GL, which nonetheless could be ordered with ABS brakes, CFC-free air conditioning, cruise control, and power glass sunroof. Most of these goodies were part of the GLS package, but the midrange Jetta also offered split folding rear seats, CD changer, and power windows. The GLX was, of course, the flagship. In addition to the VR6, the X package, still priced under $20,000, featured ABS, dual airbags, traction control, power windows, cruise control, rear spoiler, leather seats, fog lamps, and 15-inch BBS alloys. In fact, there was very little which wasn't thrown into the GLX version.

And did the Wolfsburg concern get its sums right this time? The answer was a resounding yes. Not only did the numbers figure–it was priced below all the Japanese competition–but the combination of size, space, power, and handling proved to be difficult for any manufacturer to beat, including Audi A4, Nissan Maxima, Subaru Legacy, and Acura Integra. If anything was lacking, it was perhaps ergonomics, something the Germans had

Clearly seen here is the new grille, which was part of the 1996 model year changes. This is the GL, noticeable due to the nonbody-color outside mirrors.

Face-lifts marked the 1996 Jetta. This is the Jetta GLX, with different seven-spoke alloy wheels than the earlier BBS-equipped GLX.

The GLS was a popular intermediate model, here with standard steel wheels and hubcaps. A good all-around package but lacking that very nice VR6.

been working very hard at but the Japanese had down pat. The upright Jetta, although as newly designed as its counterparts, also was much chunkier, particularly when placed next to VW's own Audi A4.

Still, the Jetta was a fine effort from VW. It hit the competition head on and came up the winner. But sales were far from what the Japanese were doing. Meanwhile, the Jetta remained unchanged from 1994 to 1995. Interestingly, a new seatbelt tensioning system was standard in 1995, which VW said, "uses a pyrotechnic device to instantly tighten belts around the front occupants in the event of a frontal impact." Between the explosions of front safety bags, side safety bags, and instant-tight belts, one may end up a victim of friendly fire in the war against accidental injury.

The three Jettas continued into 1996, but with minor trim and body modifications to provide more family identification. The GL and GLS now came standard with power-assisted rack and pinion steering and power-assisted brakes. Stereo systems by Bose were now optional.

Back at market city, the "Driver's Wanted" campaign begun in 1995 was augmented in 1997 by focusing on active (and financially viable) members of

Exciting, no? Just the thing for those who really want to go off-road. The Trek Limited Edition model, equipped with a Trek mountain bike. This is a 1996 model.

The professional mountain bike team, with a Trek Jetta. From left to right: Don Myrha, Jeff Bicknell, Miles Davis, Darryl Price, and Travis Brown. VW was being more direct in its advertising, sponsoring a number of sporting bike events.

Generation X, i.e., the kids of Baby Boomers. Fahrvergnugen, created in 1992, was out, and VW hired Arnold Fortuna Lawner & Cabot, a firm which had no automotive experience, to launch a $130 million advertising effort. VW also began to sponsor concerts on college campuses and sporting events like the San Francisco Marathon. It was working. Sales jumped 18 percent from 1995 to 1996.

In line with the new ad campaign, a limited edition model was introduced in 1996, called the Trek, which came with a custom-built Trek 21-speed mountain bike and custom roof rack. The model added fog lights, rear spoiler, style seats, and bike icons. Now, although enough research will probably prove us wrong, this is perhaps the first time a car has come equipped with a bike. (A word or two about the bike. Designed exclusively for VW, the Trek/Jetta features a double-butted chrome moly frame on 26x2.1 inch Kahuna tires. GripShift twisters link to a Shimano STX drivetrain. VW also sponsored a four-man team, which was headed for the 1996 Olympic Games.)

The effort was aimed at those with an "active life style." It was a unique marketing idea, and in 1997 led to the Jetta K2 and Jazz, special editions also

available with the hatchback Golf. The K2 version offered either a pair of El Camino skis or a Juju snowboard, both made by K2. The Jetta K2 listed at $15,995. The Jazz was a more passive edition, offering only a premium eight-speaker AM/FM cassette stereo with a six-disc CD changer. About the only

Trek Limited Edition label on the Jetta. It was much easier to spot by the Trek mountain bike sitting high up on the roof. The Trek was followed by the K2.

The Jazz, Volkswagen's third special edition of the 1997–1998 model year, which featured a six-disc CD changer and the Jazz decal on the trunklid. The alloy wheels also came with the package, which otherwise was a GLS.

other feature of the Jazz was a Jazz decal on the rear deck, and a range of special colors.

There seemed to be some reason to introduce a fourth Jetta in 1997, called the GT. It was the tried-and-true formula used with the Golf GTI/VR6 GTI.

By 1998 the Jetta line-up included something for just about everyone. This is the TDI, a diesel that wished it weren't. It was remarkably clean, however, and was good for 49 miles per gallon on the highway.

Give them just about everything in the GLX package but the engine, spruce up the interior with sport seats, and bolt on some new alloy wheels, and you've got yourself a GT, which, if we haven't forgotten, means Gran Turismo. The GL, GLS, and GLX continued as before.

In addition to the limited edition Trek, K2, and Jazz, the line up of regular models now included a GL, GT, GLS, GLX, and the TDI, which fell between the GL and GT. The TDI was the clean, fuel-efficient diesel offered in the 1996–97 Passat. In the Jetta, gas mileage, EPA-wise, was 49 miles per gallon highway and 40 miles per gallon in the city. And with a special catalytic converter, TDI models met California emissions standards, which was probably the reason for the diesel option. It surely wasn't gas consumption; in 1998, gas prices were hovering around $1.10 per gallon.

The Jetta III was well established and selling well. The line ensured there were options for everyone from the environmentalist to Gen Xers to soccer moms tired of minivans.

Chapter 24

Golf III
1993–1999

★★
1993
Golf GL

★★
1993
Golf GTI

★★★
1994–1999
Golf III Cabriolet

★★★
1995–1999
Golf GTI VR6

★★
1995–1996
Golf Sport

★★
1996–1999
Golf GTI 2.0

★★
1997–1999
Golf Trek,
K2, Jazz

The third generation of the Golf was ready for U.S. entry by 1993, and it was hoped that the Golf III would boost severely sagging sales numbers. For VW, once the undisputed foreign-car sales leader, sales had steadily declined since 1970, when over 569,000 vehicles were sold in the U.S. In 1993, the worst year ever, that number was down to a paltry 49,553. Due in part to the inherent qualities exhibited by the new Golf (and Jetta), sales increased 18.6 percent to 115,114 units from 1994 to 1996. VW wasn't sure of where it was going yet, but at least the charts had lines going in the right direction.

The Golf III had a new emphasis, not so much on performance or pizzazz, but on safety and "green" concepts. The new Golf met not only the 30-miles-per-hour front and rear crash standards, but the 35-miles-per-hour standards and side-impact requirements for the 1994 model year. On the environmental scene, VW was well on its way to the ultimate throwaway car. All post-1992 German-market Golfs can be returned to the factory, where VW will recycle the plastics, rubber, and metal once the car's road life is over.

Despite the increased strengthening, the Golf III still weighed in at around 2,500 pounds. The standard engine was the new 2.0-liter 115-horsepower, equipped with a cross-flow head. ABS was offered with ventilated discs up front and solid discs in the rear, a carryover from the GTI. Also familiar were the MacPherson struts and stabilizer bar, but with new geometry that improved stability when braking. At the rear,

Three generations of Golf: the 1979–1984 Rabbit-Golf, left; the 1985–1992 Golf, right; and the 1993 Golf, introduced to the United States in March 1993, center. This is a 1991 Euro model.

A European Golf again—this time, the GTI VR6. The body design was credited to Herbert Schafer and crew.

The 15-degree VR6 as installed in the new Golf. Clean, efficient, fast. The design, however, dates back to the Lancia narrow-angle V-4s.

the independent torsion beam axle was self-adjusting to reduce rear wheel steering. As expected, the gas mileage was good to excellent, with 32 miles per gallon on the highway and 24 in town.

Evolutionary rather than revolutionary, the new Golf kept the overall dimensions similar to the earlier model but increased interior room with an emphasis on practicality. The hatch area provided 17.5 cubic feet of space that expanded to 41 cubic feet when the rear seat was folded down, and as with the old Golf, both two-door and four-door sedans were built. Body rigidity was improved, and an automatic four-speed was optional. The GTI and GL trim packages were the only options for 1993, a year in which, according to VW, only a limited number were sold. The GTI package included CFC-free air conditioning, power glass sunroof, eight-speaker AM/FM cassette stereo, sport seats, and adjustable steering wheel.

Initially the GTI was a trim package only, with the standard eight-valve four. What it needed was the VR6, but marketing a VR6 GTI would bring it too close to the Corrado. The price would have to be less, and indications were that it would outperform the Corrado. The GTI package was officially not available during the 1994 model year as VW concentrated on the Golf GL. Priced at only $11,600, the Golf III was very competitive with the Honda Civic and Toyota Corolla, had more horsepower, and offered more overall room than most of the Japanese cars. The GL needed only a sophisticated sales strategy. In 1994, VW fired their advertising agency, Berlin Cameron Doyle. It would mark the beginning of a new ad campaign that, to date, at least, has increased VW sales in the United States.

While the U.S. media gave the Golf III a warm reception, it was hard to get excited about another econobox. Ergo, little press and no public reaction. What the Golf needed was a true GTI, and so did the press. *That* would be exciting. Thus, in 1995, as the "Driver's Wanted" jingo began to replace the foggy "Fahrvergnugen," VW dropped the Corrado, with the superb VR6, and introduced the Golf III GTI VR6.

This time the GTI was a comprehensive package, designed to outperform all rivals and yet ride as quietly and comfortably as the Passat. Right off the mark, the 0–60 time near 7 seconds was admirable,

A car for the next century. The Golf III interior reflects the softer lines of the 1990s, in contrast to the boxier look of earlier Golf dashboards. GT versions have a tach with an integrated multifunctional display in place of the clock.

A standard 1993 offering, the Golf III GL. The new Golf used the same basic engine as the Jetta III, the 2.0-liter four with 115 horsepower; 14-inch wheels were standard. The Golf III GL definitely had a chic 1990s look.

The 1993 GTI, U.S. style. With no more performance than was available with the standard GL, it did offer a close-ratio five-speed transmission and a top speed of 120 miles per hour.

and the top speed was limited to 130 miles per hour, at which time a rev limiter would come into effect. The VR6 was not only rated at a full 172 horsepower, but the power was nicely distributed over the rpm range, providing at least 85 percent of the 173 foot-pounds of torque between 2,000 and 6,000 rpm. Matched to a close-ratio five-speed gearbox, the new GTI did indeed sing. The price, fully loaded and ready to go, was just above $19,000.

To cope with the extra power, the suspension was uprated. Shocks were stiffer up front, and gas shocks were fitted to the rear. To help prevent wheelspin, an electronic traction control system controlled the front wheels, augmented by the "Plus Axle" front suspension geometry. Four-wheel ABS brakes with 11-inch ventilated discs up front, and 6 1/2x15-inch alloys with 205/50 R15H Goodyear Eagle Gas tires completed the handling package. Needless to relate that in the world of Golf, the VR6 GTI is by far the best bet for anyone looking at the Golf III range of cars.

The standard issue, bread-and butter Golf III, U.S. style. Available in either four-door or two-door, the wheelbase was the same at 97.3 inches. The engine was cast iron with an aluminum head, good for about 115 horsepower.

The first GTIs imported were flash only. But VW brought in the VR6 GTI for the 1995 model year. The 172 horsepower narrow-angle V-6 transformed the standard Golf into one of the best pocket rockets ever built.

A wide stance, color-coded moldings and bumpers, and the VR6 label on the grille make the GTI appear aggressive. Note the fog lamps incorporated into the lighting arrangement. This is a 1995 version.

The standard GL remained essentially unchanged, adding only new safety features, such as improved side-impact protection required for 1997 federal standards, and dual airbags. The CD player arrived as standard equipment, as did the CFC-free air conditioning.

A Sport option trim was new for 1995. It was, in effect, a GTI without the VR6, and could be had with just about anything the GTI offered but the power, making it necessary for the competition to spot the correct grille nomenclature before a stoplight grand prix. Is it a GTI or a Sport? The answer could only be determined by the option sheet or police radar.

Volkswagen was finally achieving the media attention so badly needed. The VR6 put the GTI, as well as the Jetta and Passat, on the map. The VR6 was selected as one of *Ward's International's* "Ten Best Engines," and winner of the *Popular Mechanics* "Design and Engineering " award. *Road & Track* described it as the "engine that just can't stop delighting us." Whatever platform, the VR6 transformed the product and elicited rave reviews from the press.

But how did the GTI VR6 fare with the competition? The 1996 version, with a new leather seat option, subtle handling improvements such as stiffer (yet) shocks, and lowered by 10 millimeters in front, was pitted against the new BMW 318ti hatchback in a *Road & Track* comparison test. It was a draw, but side-by-side comparisons on the slalom, skid pad, and race track revealed that the GTI chassis was not up to that of the BMW. Conversely, the VR6-equipped GTI outpowered the BMW's 138-horsepower twin-cam 16-valve four. The GTI did the quarter-mile in 15.6 seconds, hitting 100 miles per

The 1996 VR6 GTI sported 6 1/2x15-inch five-spoke wheels. This differentiated it from the GTI 2.0 which was also offered that year. The GTI VR6 is also 10 millimeters lower than previous models.

The success of the GTI VR6 led VW to market another GTI, but without the VR6. This 1996 GTI had the same, robust but pedestrian 115-horsepower 2.0 four as the GL. The wheels are 6x14 versus the 6½x15 used by the GTI VR6.

Minor trim differences in the 1997 GL model include a slightly redesigned grille and airdam. Emphasis was on safety and practicality. The Golf success was reflected in a VW sales increase of 18 percent from 1995 to 1996.

The GTI 2.0 in 1997 guise. The trim package included sport front seats, a GTI lookalike grille, and roof-mounted antenna. The 14-inch alloys gave it away, however. The GTI could do 0–60 in about 9 seconds.

For 1998, the Golf line continued to offer three base variations: the GL, seen here; the GTI; and the GTI VR6. The Golf III always looked strong and safe, due to the thick door pillars. The GL line continues to be the Golf price leader for 1998 and beyond.

hour before the BMW hit 90 miles per hour. But the Bimmer cost more, too, by about $4,000. All together, a remarkable feat for VW.

Taking advantage of the good press, VW decided to rename the Sport to GTI, still with the nominal 115-horsepower four. Performance wasn't bad, though, with 0–60 times of about 9 seconds. The only thing missing was that wonderful engine, the VR6 emblem on the grille, smaller wheels, and an inch off the 11-inch VR6 front discs. Bringing up the rear was the GL, established as a price leader, which soldiered along admirably, getting new standard cloth seats and a full-size glovebox.

In 1996, the Jetta introduced the Trek, complete with a custom-built Trek bike sitting astride the roof, and in 1997 the same marketing ploy was applied to the Golf. The Trek version was tagged at $14,350. In addition to the Trek, the Golf range included the K2 and Jazz, options also available on the Jetta.

The formula appeared to be working, sales continued to rise, and at least the GTI had a presence, and now, an increasingly good reputation. "If it's not broke

1998 GTI VR6 is seen here with another variation of the alloy wheels, these even more aggressive than before. Note the small "VR6" badge under the GTI label. Radio frequency locking was new with the 1998 models.

The GTI for 1998 remained essentially unchanged, but could now be ordered in "Jazz blue" and yellow. Accented red trim in the interior lent a colorful touch to the otherwise straight-laced Germanic interiors.

The Jetta Trek Limited Edition was followed by the Golf Trek in 1997. VW was aiming at a younger, more active generation. The stand and the Trek bike were designed specifically for Volkswagen.

The K2 special edition followed the Trek, and again was offered on both the Golf and Jetta. The buyer got a choice of either K2 skis or snowboard. Alloys were part of the package.

The 1995 Golf III Cabriolet came with a long list of standard features, including an adjustable height steering column, power windows, beverage holders, and an eight-speaker stereo. Optional were the alloy wheels, as shown, and CD changer.

don't fix it," so for the 1997 and 1998 model year there were virtually no changes in the Golf III line-up. In 1998, the GTI interior was upgraded and in addition to the black leather seat option, "GTI" emblem front seats with woven cloth accented in red trim were the standard interior. The red accent was used throughout the interior, including the shift knob, and with red seams on the handbrake, steering wheel, and shift boot.

Golf III Cabriolet

As the original VW Beetle Cabriolet had been successfully superseded by the Rabbit/Golf Cabriolet in 1980, the Karmann-built Golf was replaced by the

Golf III Cabriolet in 1994. Since the inception of the boxy but attractive Rabbit Cabriolet, the model had achieved a reputation as a young woman's car, and not without reason, as over 70 percent of the Cabrio's buyers are women.

Dates here are tricky. The Classic Golf Cabriolet was a 1993 package, which celebrated 37 consecutive years of VW cabriolets. The new Golf III Cabrio, promised for 1994, did not appear until very late in the year for the 1995 model year.

Like its predecessors, the new Golf III Cab was built in Osnabrück, and Karmann was again responsible for construction. (All other Golfs destined for the U.S. were built in Puebla, Mexico.) For the Golf III, Karmann increased chassis structural rigidity by 20 percent over the old Golf, strengthening the platform in the dashboard, bulkhead, and floor areas. A newly designed rollbar served to support side glass and allow anchor points for seatbelts, and the roll bar was responsible for a good bit of the 20 percent increase in rigidity. VW also worked on interior space, and the new Cabrio was a full four-seater with more room than the BMW 318I Convertible. Trunk space, a sore point with the old Golf, was now 33 percent larger, which was a good thing because there was so very little storage space inside the Cabrio. The top was still a one-person affair, but one had to stand outside the car to get it fully in place. As before, the six-layer top equipped with real heated glass was a masterpiece, hand-fitted at the factory. And, as before, it was expensive if repairs or replacement loomed.

Overall, the new Golf Cab was softer in line, yet again attractive, or perhaps we should say "cute." The rest of the package was almost pure GL. The standard

2.0-liter engine was the only engine available, and suspension was also standard, despite a 250-pound weight increase. Acceleration was, well, adequate. The Cabrio would get to 60 miles per hour in about 10 seconds; add another 8 seconds for the quarter-mile.

VW had also been busy at work on safety initiatives throughout the model line-up, and the Cabrio was no exception. Standard safety features included dual passenger airbags (which meant the loss of the front glove compartment), ABS brakes, improved front and rear crush zones, and 1997-standards side-impact protection.

Colors, very important to the targeted clientele, were white, red, and black in nonmetallics, and blue, violet, and green in metallics. Interiors were either black or beige, whether or not the optional "partial leather" option was ordered. In 1996, a new metallic color, Cinnabar, was added. A central power locking system, which provided the owner about a dozen ways to lock, unlock, open, and close every aperture on the car was a standard feature. As nice as these touches are, time and weather are not kind to such electro-mechanical devices; it will be interesting to see how desirable these remain after five years. Certainly locking/automatic window operation is another critical checkoff item on the used-car buyer's list. The 1995–96 Cabriolet prices ranged from just a base price of $19,975 to $23,000 fully loaded and ready to go.

There were virtually no changes for 1996. This 1997 model displays the Cabrio model with alloy-like hubcabs. Rear vision seems improved from the earlier Golf Cabrios.

VW reduced that base price to $17,925 in 1997, but added a new model, the Highline, again reflecting European nomenclature also used on the Polo. The Highline came standard with partial leather upholstery, ABS brakes, alloy wheels, body color moldings, and fog lamps. ABS was not an op-

A one-year model, the Highline, included a full option package. Leather steering wheel, door panels, and shift knob in black or beige added a nice touch. Seen here are the seven-spoke alloys with center hubcaps.

tion with the standard Cabrio. Tops now were available in cloth or vinyl.

When there are few changes in the line-up, marketing turns to name changes. The Highline model of 1997 became, with the addition of an electrically operated top, the GLS, while the base Cabrio remained just that. Side-impact airbags provided an additional option.

The Cabrio, like all platforms, could be improved by the use of the VR6. Whether or not this will be considered with a new generation of Golf Cabrios remains to be seen.

Left
The VW Cabrio Highline interior. Front seats are equipped with keep-your-buns-warm heaters, leather inserts. Note two of the eight speakers, which enabled the Spice Girls to be heard at Interstate speeds with the top down.

The soft lines of the Cabrio are even more evident with the six-layer top up. For 1998 the top was electrically operated on the GLS. The GLS offered the same options as the Highline of 1997. A VR6 would have been nice.

Chapter 25

Passat 1998–1999

Today it is difficult to build a bad car. The Japanese, having raised the bar, kept on raising it, while American and European carmakers struggled to keep up. Every new model introduced had to be right the first time, if it was to succeed in the marketplace. Build quality, materials, reliability, safety, maintenance, and economy were not only equally important, but had to be achieved at the highest levels possible.

The 1988–97 Passat was more than acceptable in most regards, but the third iteration of the Passat had to be a success right out of the box. There was no room for error, given the highly competitive market segment of the midsize sedan–a haven for Honda Accord and Ford Taurus. In Europe, the new Passat would compete against the likes of the C class Mercedes and 3 series BMW. Volkswagen again turned to Audi, this time not only for the platform but the engine and drivetrain as well. The new Passat was based on the successful Audi A4 chassis, but lengthened by 6.1 inches, 3 of which were in the wheelbase. The overall result was a car with more room than the A4 at a lower price. The new Passat was larger in all respects than the old one, and with a 106.4-inch wheelbase, it could easily accommodate five passengers. It looked like a winner, and as usual, the Passat had been available in Europe one year prior to U.S. introduction. The Passat was a success in Europe, and VW

The new Passat turned the engine around again. The VR6, used so effectively in the earlier Passats, won't fit into the new Passat. The Audi V-6 will, however, and with 200 horsepower on tap, promises to be a real autobahner.

fully expected that the Passat sales would be doubled that of the old Passat within a year.

Mechanically, the VW Passat was identical to the Audi, using the five-valve four-cylinder 1.8-liter turbocharged engine, which produced 150 horsepower at 5,700 rpm with a nice torque curve that produced 155 foot-pounds of torque from 1,750 rpm to 4,600 rpm. Like the earlier Audi-based Passat, the engine was longitudinally mounted rather than Falia's transverse arrangement. The first Passats had no engine options, and the V-6 which would later be offered was the Audi unit rather than the VW VR6. But the four was no slouch. Getting to 60 took only 8.2 seconds, and the quarter-mile took 16.3 seconds, better than the V-6-equipped Ford Taurus or the V-6 Camry. It was smooth, quiet, and efficient, enabling the Passat to record 23/32 miles per gallon EPA city/highway figures.

The suspension, too, was Audi, incorporating the four-link design, which virtually eliminated torque steer characteristics. At the rear, the track-correcting torsion beam rear axle kept the wheels parallel with each other. The handling was not as crisp as the A4's; the heavier and longer Passat was more luxury than sport. Brakes were the 11-inch ventilated units in front, 9.6-inch discs at the rear with power-assist. ABS was standard.

In general, there was high praise for the car, despite its acknowledged similarity to the Audi. The aerodynamic lines (.027 drag coefficient), which looked good on the A4/A6, suffered a bit due to the longer wheelbase. But the quality was there. The Passat was the first VW to be fully galvanized, and VW offered a limited corrosion warranty of 11 years with no mileage restrictions. An aluminum casting, or "cubing model" of the car was made and used to check gaps and joint lines with the production line. Chassis and bodyshell strength was increased 10 percent over the old Passat. Laser-beam welding and high-strength adhesives were used on the joints. Overall structural stiffness was increased 35 percent over the old Passat.

All this added to the remarkable quietness of the new Passat. The engine never seemed strained, if one could hear it at all. Wind noise was virtually eliminated due to a great amount of detail work on the design. *Autoweek* found owner's comments were positive: ". . . build quality is rock solid with no squeaks or rattles ..." "...so smooth and quiet it's easy to catch myself going way over the speed limit ..." "... the 1.8 turbo with the five speed is a wonderful combination in this car ...." *Road & Track* said that "...Volkswagen has taken an impressive first stab at reinventing itself with this roomy, refined sedan."

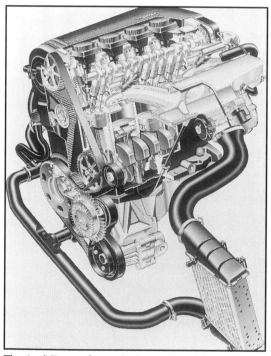

The Audi/Passat four-cylinder engine. Alloy twin-cam cross-flow head, five valves per cylinder and intercooled turbocharger create 150 very usable horses.

The standard velour interior of the 1998 Passat. The leather trim option will get you leather door panels, seat inserts, steering wheel cover, and brake and shift boots.

The 1998 Passat was introduced in GLS guise only—no alloy wheel options. The design is crisp, modern, and aerodynamic, with very little wind noise. A true five-seater, the Passat is the biggest Volks yet.

If those wheels look big, they are; 6Jx15s, in fact, but steel with wheel covers. The 1998 Passat seems fore-shortened here. The wheelbase is longer than it looks.

VW has been criticized for poor ergonomics in the past. The solution was to learn from the Japanese, with a very Honda-like dashboard. Note the foot rest on the driver's left.

So, what exactly did VW offer with the new Passat? First, there was only one model offered for 1998, the GLS. No engine options, so we start with the turbo four. The standard gearbox was a five-speed unit, and optional was the straight line shifting Tiptronic five-speed semi-automatic, which was fun if shifted manually. Traction control, which engaged selective brake application at speeds up to 24 miles per hour, was standard. The GLS came with 6Jx15-inch steel wheels with covers (no alloy option) on P195/65 R15H radials. The exterior standard features on the GLS covered just about everything one came to expect from a midrange VW option: body color bumpers and mirrors, tinted glass, daytime running lights, and metallic paint, but a power sunroof was part of a limited option package. Inside, the seats were velour, but leather inserts were optional, as was a leather-covered steering wheel. Aside from the leather, the only other option for the inside was a six-disc CD changer, which was in the 15-cubic-foot trunk anyway. But the list of standard items on the GLS was comprehensive and included side-mounted airbags in addition to front driver and passenger airbags, power windows, and central locking system. Base price was $21,530 fully loaded.

Though the standard items were more than adequate, the Passat needed some real options by the end of the year. Planned to be introduced for 1999 is the Passat station wagon, again already popular in Europe, the TDI variant for those who just have to have a diesel, and finally the Audi-based 200-horsepower, 30-valve 2.8-liter V-6.

Chapter 26

New Beetle 1998–1999

★★★★
1998–1999
New Beetle

Cool from the outside, warm on the inside. Driving the New Beetle in winter will be comfortable with the Golf heater. And it will be some time before the design stops eliciting "cool" comments from onlookers.

The New Beetle is, on one hand, a statement about a successful if troublesome past; on the other, it is an exclamation about a bold, innovative, and bright future.

Never mind that the New Beetle is just a Golf in a jellybean. Never mind that the final product was light years away from what the designers–American, by the way–had in mind. And never mind that at first the boys from Wolfsburg didn't want anything to do with a new Beetle. It would, perhaps, remind Germans of a time they'd rather forget. Never mind that VW was not the first major manufacturer to produce a retro-car based on an earlier product; as early as 1965, Alfa Romeo turned out the 1750 Gran Sport, a faithful but modern version of the immortal 1932 1750. We can forget the dubious attempt to use the Bea-

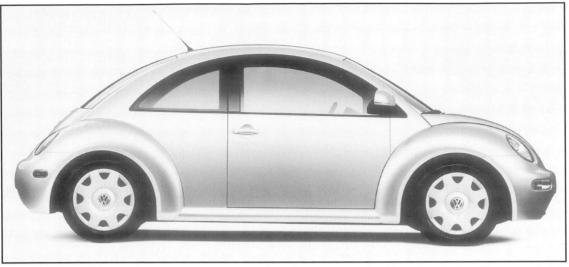

Not nearly as clean as the Concept One introduced at Detroit, the New Beetle is still a remarkable achievement in light of the use of the existing Golf platform. From the A-pillar forward, the lines are slightly uncomfortable. Overall, however, it works.

tles to sell Beetles. VW hoped that the Beetle "would evoke memories of the Woodstock era" and thought the Beatles would fit well with this strategy. The Beatles didn't.

All of this aside, the New Beetle was the automotive sensation of 1998.

The New Beetle had its origins in California, where VW has a design studio. The New Beetle design, called Concept One, was based on the Polo chassis, and by utilizing a hybrid electrical drive, would meet the California Zero Emissions Standards. Plans

From the rear, the New Beetle is most pleasing. The VW emblem is also the latch for the trunk. No engine there, as many have thought. That would be retrograde.

called for the car to be offered with the TDI diesel and a pure electric drive as well. The prototype was smooth and clean, effectively aerodynamic while at the same time declaring very clearly that it was a Volkswagen Beetle. Volkswagen decided to show it at the Detroit Auto Show in 1994. To say it was a hit is an understatement. But as VW started development of a production prototype, several decisions had to be made. The electric-hybrid idea was instant history, and as the Polo chassis wasn't U.S.-certified, the New Beetle would have to be based on the Golf chassis. After driving the outsourced prototype, VW boss Ferdinand Piech decided that to be done right, it would have to be done at VW in Wolfsburg rather than with outsiders. Once Piech was behind the project, it was completed in a remarkably short time.

But, as we said, what we have here is a Golf. The platform, insofar as production welding points go, is identical to the 1999 Golf, as are the engine and engine options, transmission, interior dimensions, and overall dimensions. But using the Golf chassis meant that production could begin sooner and without a great deal of extra cost.

A further benefit in using the Golf platform was the ability to offer existing engine options: the 2.0-liter gas four used in the basic Golf, the TDI diesel as offered with Jetta, and finally the 150-horsepower turbo four, which wouldn't be ready until 1999. As the Golf is currently produced in Mexico, it made sense to also produce the New Beetle there. Note, however, the New Beetle is based not on the existing Golf platform, but the 1999 Golf, which was already in production in Europe. The differences are minor; the wheelbase is increased from 97.4 inches to 98.9 inches, the front track increased from 57.5 inches to 59.6 inches, and at the rear from 57 inches to 58.7 inches. The coil-over-shock arrangement used on the rear suspension of the old Golf has given way to separate shocks and coil springs. According to latest reports at press time, about 60,000 New Beetles will be built yearly, with 40,000 scheduled for the United States.

The New Beetle was making good press. In fact, no Volkswagen ever made such a splash in the nation's media, both general and automotive. No one, not even the often acerbic Jean Lindamood Jennings of *Automobile,* had a bad word for the car. It was voted Best of the Best in Show by *AutoWeek,* winning over the BMW Z07 supercar and the Porsche 911 Cabriolet. Every major network and newspaper ran features. The New Beetle firmly put Volkswagen back on the map, and suddenly the days of media malaise were over. *Everyone* took notice. Ironically, the press could have been unkind. Environmentalists could have claimed the car was a major cop-out and that the electric-hybrid powerplant should have been retained. Others could have pointed out that the New Beetle was a cheap shot, an ugly duckling capitalizing on the past. Still others might have claimed that for all the noise, the New Beetle did not offer one technological breakthrough or improvement. But they didn't, probably swayed by a remarkable tide of public interest.

Like its more conservative relatives, the New Beetle came with a huge list of standard items: tach, six-speaker stereo cassette, dual airbags, clock, floormats, the central locking system, and power door locks. Options will eventually include a sunroof

The headlights, windshield, emblem, and openings mimic the rear of the New Beetle. No one has yet joked about it coming or going. The bumpers, both front and rear, are extremely well integrated into the design.

(1999); leather seating; cold-weather kit, which provides heated front seats, and washer nozzles. U.S. cars were delivered with the Sport and Convenience Option package which included the 16-inch alloy wheels, fog lights, cruise control and power windows. Brakes, upgraded by Piech to include discs on the rear, had 10-inch ventilated discs in front. Standard wheels were the 61/2Jx16 steel wheels with covers, and six-spoke alloy wheels of the same size were optional. Many failed to notice the 16-inch wheels; it had been over 47 years since Volkswagen last had such large wheels, and they were on the original Type 1 sedan. Others never realized that the much-heralded flower vase did not stem from Haight-Ashbury but was an option on the 1952–53 Beetles, along with luxurious back seat pillows. Offered colors were white, red, black, and yellow in nonmetallic, and silver, blue, green, and dark blue in metallic. And while the old VW was instrument-poor, the New Beetle featured a tach, engine temperature gauge, and a fuel gauge. For those who were looking for the auxiliary fuel tank spigot, there was none.

On first sight, the New Beetle seems to be larger and bulkier than the 1200/1300s of the mid-1960s. It is deceptive. The New Beetle is just about the same height (59.5 inches) as the original, but the overall length of 161.1 inches is more than 5 inches *shorter* but the wheelbase for the New Beetle

The now famous bud vase (not a receptacle for a beer) is almost lost in the vast expanse of dashboard, which just keeps on going and going and going. Washing the inside of the windshield will not be a popular pastime.

is 4 inches longer than the old. It is the extra width that is most noticeable; the New Beetle is a full 7 inches wider than the rear-engined car. That accounts for the extra living space offered by the New Beetle, and contributes to handling characteristics only dreamt of by the People's Car. The 1999 New Beetle is almost 1,000 pounds heavier than the 1,760 pounds of the 1965 version, but with 65 more horsepower, the New Beetle outperforms all variations of the flat four-powered cars. What had not improved was the miles per gallon. The gas version still achieves only 22–29 miles per gallon, almost exactly what the 1300 VW did for *Road & Track* in 1965. Lastly, comparisons pale when price is discussed. The 1300 sold for $1,900 fully equipped in 1965; the New Beetle, with the 115-horsepower gas engine and five-speed was intro-

Yes, this is a Golf, but it is hard to imagine either from the outside or from the inside. The interior is a charming blend of old and new ideas. The steering wheel, instruments, gearshift, and cabin shape work well with the overall concept.

Sixteen-inch wheels, first used on the original Type 1, are not as obvious to the eye as one might think. 6 1/2Jx16 wheel sizes were offered on both the standard steel wheel and the optional six-spoke alloys. Tires were P205/55 R16 in either case.

Not much room to maneuver in the tight engine bay. The plastic cover is easily removable for access to plugs and fuel injection. The 115-horsepower engine allows more than acceptable performance, but the 155-horsepower version for 1999 will really move it.

duced at the dealers with a sticker price of just over $17,000. Some things do change.

It was, we thought, smart to wait some weeks after the New Beetle hit the showroom to get a chance to drive a demo. Three weeks after it arrived, on a wet and dreary Saturday at 5 P.M., we made our way to

In the right-hand corner is the tach. To the left is the gas gauge. Mileage indicators are digital. A nice arrangement, lit in astro blue.

the local dealer, Fairfax Imports Inc. of Fairfax, Virginia. There were three demos on the lot, and dozens of potential buyers simply crawling all over the cars, forgetting the time and weather. So much for waiting for the crowds to thin out. Salesman Larry Schiro greeted us. "It gets worse as the TV ads appear and more cars are seen on the road," Larry said. "I have been selling VWs for eight years and have never, ever, seen anything like this. On the road, people will follow the Beetle until the salesperson stops or arrives at the dealership. The entire police force has been by to look at the car. So has the fire department. There are always people waiting in line to drive one." But, The New Beetle is both a salesperson's dream and nightmare. Schiro had no cars in stock that were not already sold, and he had just been told that his dealership, one of the largest on the East Coast, would be allocated only 225 New Beetles this year.

Few cars could claim such widespread public enthusiasm. Perhaps the 1953 Corvette or the 1961 XKE, but both were exotics. Perhaps the 1964 Mustang, but nothing much in recent memory. But, the New Beetle has won the hearts of a large segment of

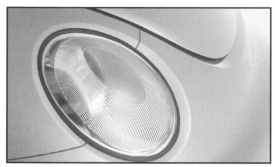

Front headlights also incorporate daytime running lights. They are also very reminiscent of the pre-1967 Beetle's covered headlights, which gave way to standard sealed-beam units. Today's headlights are one of the more decorative items on an automobile.

Door panel of the New Beetle is thoroughly modern. The power windows have one-touch control and an "anti-pinch" safety device, stopping immediately when resistance is met during the upward climb. Oh, yes, six speakers are standard in U.S. trim.

the overall population, and of course, it is still affordable (although prices, with the automatic and dealer prep are edging towards $19,000, and 1999 Beetles with the sunroof may break the $20,000 mark). And they are visiting the showroom in unheard of numbers. Volkswagen thought that the New Beetle would be a low-volume "niche market" item. We don't think so. VW has also created a speculation market by not being able to fulfill the demand soon enough.

Schiro did strongarm a five-speed demo for us, although the run was very brief–we were holding up others who also wanted a drive. On the road, it is very Golf-like, but the small wheel (fully adjustable) and imaginative interior allows one to soon forget the Golf associations. There is no Beetle-like engine noise, but the transverse four of the New Beetle definitely makes itself heard. As expected, visibility is great, and ergonomically the driving position and switches are fine, but the rearview mirror and sunshades are a bit of a reach. The tach is very small and unobtrusively placed, and therefore not always used. The 2-plus feet of dash and total drop-off in front take some getting used to. The handling is quick and responsive, thanks to the 16-inch low-profile alloy wheels. The gearshift linkage is a bit vague, feeling too loose, and the clutch is light without much feel. Nevertheless, it was fun to drive, and that is really the name of the game here. And the bud vase? Larry puts a new flower in every one he sells.

So why four stars? Because finally VW is paying attention to the *desires*–not necessarily the needs–of the American market. And because, like the Plymouth Prowler (a retro car fortunately *not* based on an old Plymouth), it is smart retro–cute but eminently more usable than the Prowler. Because it put VW on the map again after years in the doldrums. And because it was greeted with such great interest when it arrived in March of 1998. Is it too bad VW had to capitalize on the past? Perhaps, but everybody does, including Mercedes-Benz and BMW. It rates four stars simply because *it is*.

Chapter 27

Around the Bend

The next edition of the *Illustrated Volkswagen Buyer's Guide* could feature a cover with a luxury car, Formula One race car, or a high-tech super car. The days of the Beetle, New or old, will be merely reminders of a day long past. Volkswagen is aggressively on the move toward a totally new environment. In 1998, with a flurry of activity that set the automotive world upside down, Volkswagen/Audi boldly purchased Cosworth Engineering, Rolls Royce, and Lamborghini. Obviously, because of this unification, the possibilities are endless: from a Cosworth-engined mass-produced Rolls Royce to a W12-powered Lambo. In addition, VW announced plans to build a Sport Ute with Porsche. While speculation ran rampant regarding overall design, it was clear that the VW-Porsche SUV would be headed for the United States as soon as possible. But during the hype and excitement of mid-1998, improvements and additions to the bread-and-butter model line-up were being announced, with all four wheels firmly on the ground.

The Passat Plus

The 1998 Passat borrowed very heavily from Audi, and put the top-of-the-line model up yet another notch, edging ever closer to the products from Stuttgart and Munich. No sooner had the 1998 Passat hit the

The New Golf as introduced in Germany for the 1999 model year. It is a refined and more attractive Golf III. Note the steep rake of the windshield and the less-obtrusive door pillars. Still, no doubt that this is a VW Golf.

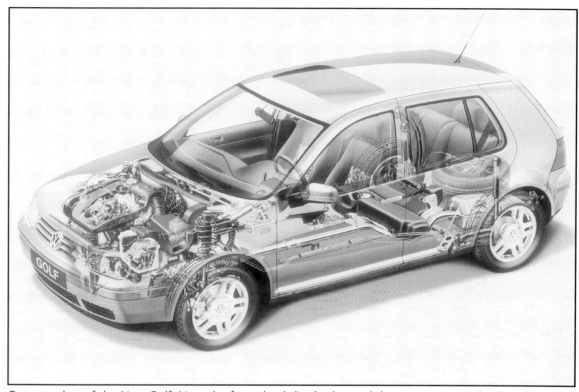

Cutaway shot of the New Golf. Note the four-wheel disc brakes and the now-separate shocks and springs on the rear suspension. Front discs are ventilated, and overall suspension is improved

showrooms when the Passat Plus was announced. With another 3 inches added to the wheelbase, the Plus will be powered by a 300-horsepower W8 engine of 3.8 liters. The W8 is similar to the WR12, but based on two siamesed 1.9-liter V-4s, also new. Plans are also under way for an SUV, surely aimed at the lucrative U.S. market. The Golf and Jetta will be replaced in 1999, and a new Golf Cabriolet is slotted for introduction in 2001.

The New Golf

Late in 1997, for the 1998 model year, VW introduced the fourth generation of Golf, but this time sans the roman numerals. It should appear in the United States in the 1999 model year. It was simply called the "new" Golf, and for the most part was a continuation of the Golf III theme. The new Golf shares the same platform as the New Beetle (see New Beetle chapter), and while easily recognizable as a Golf, with a drag coefficient of only 0.31, it is more aerodynamic than the Golf III. The windshield is raked back and, with less-prominent A- and B- pil-

lars, makes the new Golf a much better-looking econobox. Econobox is no longer an apt description, because the new Golf offers luxury, safety, and convenience items not generally associated with economy. The new dash features the same blue lighting as does the New Beetle; the steering wheel is adjustable for reach *and* angle; and the driver's seat is infinitely variable. Options will include an antidazzle rearview mirror and a rain sensor that automatically switches on the wipers at the first signs of rain. This is in addition to the many features already in place on the Golf III.

Perhaps the most interesting options available–at least in Europe–are the radio navigation system (the first on a compact-class car) and the Emergency Telematic system. The navigation system uses the Global Positioning System (GPS) in conjunction with the VW multifunction display located in the central console, and is capable of displaying detailed maps. It also includes a Traffic Information Memory which can calculate and display alternative routes based on traffic information bulletins.

Combining the advantages of GPS and a car phone, the Telematic Service makes it possible to receive traffic information as well as use phone features in case of an emergency or breakdown. The mobile phone requests up-to-the-minute traffic information, and if a breakdown is experienced, the systems will send a message to the traffic control center (remember, this is in Germany) that includes all information necessary to get help.

The GTI version is alive and well and now comes with Recaro seats and those neat 16-inch wheels with 205/55 R tires. In Europe, the GTI is available with three engines: a 150-horsepower 1.8 Turbo with five valves per cylinder, a new V-5 displacing 2.3 liters with 150 horsepower, and finally a 1.9-liter 110-horsepower diesel. These are among eight Golf engine options available in Europe. It is not clear which engines will power stateside Golfs.

Not content with just going after the luxury car market while introducing new compact-class models, they are also concentrating on the huge minicar segment in Europe. VW will introduce what is now called the Lupo (watch for a name change on that one), a car even smaller than the current Polo. A fuel-

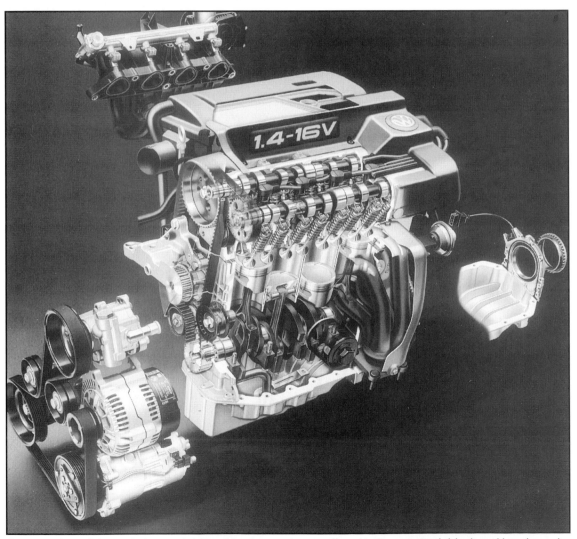

Cutaway shot of the entirely new 1.4-liter 16-valve engine as offered in Europe. Both block and head are aluminum. This version produces 75 horsepower, but probably won't be available in the U.S.

efficient version may be called the Lupino and will get 94 miles per gallon. In total, VW is expecting sales to improve by at least six million per year (worldwide) by the year 2003, trailing only GM and Ford.

The WR12 Sports Cars

Perhaps the most startling initiatives have been the show cars–another PR effort not historically used by Volkswagen. Both the coupe introduced at Tokyo in late 1997 and the sports car first shown at Geneva in early 1998 provide wildly attractive showcases for the WR12 engine. But by June of 1998, Volkswagen had purchased the ailing Lamborghini company, and the effects of this purchase on the fate of the WR12 cars is unknown.

Yet the Ital Design (a.k.a. Fabrizio Giugiaro) WR12 Sport Coupe was no idle threat. Piech was quoted as saying that the coupe is "no joke" and the WR12 will power a sports car. He has also confirmed that VW will build 200 coupes and 100 roadsters, but it was not clear if any would be imported to the United States.

The coupe featured a monocoque frame with front-hinged upward-swinging doors, à la Lamborghini

Countach. Weighing in at only 2,600 pounds, the carbon-fiber body was only 42 inches high, 173 inches long, and 75 inches wide. Its Italian parentage was obvious, and it looks every inch a threat to Ferrari.

More aggressive than the Ferrari 355, yet less outrageous than the Lambo Diablo, the VW coupe

Dashboard of New Golf is softer, less cluttered, and, as in other new VW products, the VW emblem is loud and clear. Instruments are lit in a very attractive blue. The center console will also house the new GPS-based navigation system.

There is no doubt that this is a supercar. That this is also a Volkswagen (without assistance from Porsche or Audi) is a revelation. VW went to Ital Design for the bodywork, and probably production, but the WR12 engine was VW twice over.

Maranello, meet Wolfsburg. Note the large VW emblems on the front and rear. Those are meaty 19-inch wheels shod with 285/35ZRs on the rear. Piech says 200 will be made, but no price or U.S. availability at press time.

comes off very well as a fully modern supercar. Price will no doubt be less than either of the Italians.

The engine, however, was as Teutonic as Wotan. Two VR6 engines were joined at a 72-degree angle, sharing a seven-bearing crankshaft, in an aluminum crankcase. Four valves per cylinder are operated by four overhead *chain-driven* cams–which will probably make it sound like early Italian primitives. The 5.6-liter engine produces about 420 horsepower, or so it was reported at the time. Placed longitudinally in the chassis, it was mated to a six-speed gearbox driving a viscous coupling to distribute power to both front and rear wheels.

The same concept was employed with the roadster, called "the sports car" for its Geneva introduction. Strangely, in neither case were the cars given any particular nomenclature, although they screamed to be called something else than VW sports cars. Perhaps

that is OK. The name callers at VW never have been as gifted as the engineers. And a rose by any other name . . .

As we come to the close of this particular chapter of the history of Volkswagen, it is gratifying to observe the tremendous strides VW has taken since 1993–the year in which the first edition of the *Illustrated Volkswagen Buyer's Guide* was published. In fact 1993 was the worst year in the company's long life, and yet under Ferdinand Piech, Volkswagen has transformed itself from a has-been to a will-be. It is almost impossible to keep up with the exciting and rapid changes occurring within Wolfsburg. They have delighted the enthusiasts, comforted the traditionalists, kept up with the generations, pacified the environmentalists, and continue to produce and sell excellent products at all levels. One can ask no more from a producer of automobiles.

The steering wheel looks familiar, although the production model will probably have a less extravagant dashboard. VW emblems are, again, very prominent, and yet they appear strangely out of place in a supercar. But we can get used to anything when it comes in a package like this.

Left
VW had come up with a winner in the VR6, which was widely acclaimed. Then why not double it, called it the WR12, and install it in a four-wheel-drive supercar? There is a good deal of engineering here, however. Putting two engines together is rarely easy, nor often very successful.

Index

Boano, Mario Felice, 47
Denzel, Wolfgang, 56
Devin, Bill, 56
Doyle Dane Bernbach, 26, 31, 49
Exner, Virgil, 47
Feuereissen, Dr. Karl, 14
Ganz, Josef, 12
Hirst, Major Ivan, 41
Hitler, Adolph, 12
Hoffman, Max, 16
Holste, Werner, 81
Karmann, Dr. Wilhelm, Jr., 47
Karmann, Wilhelm, Sr., 42
Klaue, Hermann, 78
Kraus, Ludwig, 82
Leiding, Rudolf, 82
Lotz, Kurt, 81

Models
    Beetle Convertible, 41–46
    Beetle New 163–169
    Beetle Sedan, 5–8, 12–33
    Beetle Sedan deluxe, 15, 16, 19
    Corrado, 128–132
    Dasher (Passat), 82, 83
    EuroVan, 66, 67
    Fox, 83
    Fox Polo, 83
    Gold Syncro, 108. 109
    Golf, 122–127
    Golf III, 147–158
    Golf III Cabriolet, 156–158
    Golf, New, 171–173
    Golf Rallye, 109
    Jetta, 116–121
    Jetta II, 118
    Jetta III, 141–146
    K70, 81, 82
    Karmann-Ghia, 47–53
    Kübelwagen, 68–71
    Kombi, 58–66
    Microbus, 58–66
    Microbus Deluxe, 59, 60
    Passat, 133–140, 159–162
    Passat Plus, 170, 171

Polo, 94–96
Quantum, 112–115
Quantum Syncro, 110, 111
Rabbit (Golf), 84–93
Schwimmwagen, 68–71
Scirocco, 97–105
Sports Bug, 35, 36, 40
Super Beetle, 34–40
Thing, The, 71, 72
Transporter, 58–66
Type 1 special-bodied cars
    Dannenhauser, 56
    Denzel, 56
    Devin, 56
    Enzmann, 56
    Hebmüller, 54, 55
    MCA Jetstar, 56
    Replicars, 56, 57
    Rometsch, 55, 56
    Stauss, Eller, Drews, 56
Type 2, 29
Type 3, 28, 29, 73–77
Type 4, 78–80
Type 11, 13
Type 13, 13
Type 14, 13
Type 15, 13, 43
Type 82, 69
Type 82E, 69, 70
Type 87, 69
Type 113, 34
Type 128, 69
Type 143, 49
Type 166, 69–71
Type 181, 71, 72
Vanagon, 58–66
Vanagon Syncro, 107–109
WR12 Sports Cars, 173, 174
Nordhoff, Heinz, 14–16, 34, 73, 74, 78
Pon, Ben, 21, 58
Porsche, Ferdinand, 12
Porsche, Ferry, 13
Radclyffe, Colonel C. R., 41
Reimspiess, Francis Xaver, 13
Reuters, Ernst, 43